How to organize a·local collection

How to organize a local collection

Alice Lynes

(formerly Librarian, Coventry and
Warwickshire Collection, Coventry City Libraries)

Grafton Basic Text
Editor: Evelyn J. A. Evans, CBE, FLA

 ANDRE DEUTSCH/A Grafton Book

First published 1974 by
André Deutsch Limited
105 Great Russell Street London WC1

Printed in Great Britain by
Ebenezer Baylis and Son Limited
The Trinity Press Worcester and London

ISBN 0 233 96452 5

Contents

Contents

Preface

The growth of interest in local studies, particularly since the last war, combined with new methods and materials of historical research, have given public libraries an increasing responsibility to provide the means for such study. Many have expanded and reorganized their local collections, and it was in such an exercise that I became involved. Coventry had a fine collection of local material, almost totally unorganized; it had suffered some grievous wartime losses and had spent six years in boxes at an outlying branch library. For no other apparent reasons than being a native Coventrian, almost the 'oldest inhabitant' on the staff and known to be willing to 'have a go' at most things, I found myself with the job of building this into a working collection to meet the widely varying requirements of the general public, to whom it was, for the first time, to be made available. With no specialist training for the work, make-shift premises and little money, it was largely a matter of improvisation; some of the practices evolved may not measure up to the highest standards of the profession, but they made the department 'tick' to good effect.

What I have written about the organization of a local collection is based entirely on the experience of creating a department of generally acknowledged worth. I have tried to cover all aspects of local collection work and I hope that some of the things I learned the hard way may prove useful to others similarly situated, if only to suggest to them improvements.

Writing in retirement, when I was no longer in daily contact with the subject, presented some difficulties which were overcome by the generous co-operation of others. Miss Virginia Gilbert, my successor in the Coventry and Warwickshire Collection, was always at the other end of the telephone to provide an answer to the many queries that cropped up; equally helpful were other members of the staff of Coventry City Libraries, Museums and Art Gallery. To my cousin, Alice Saunders, I am deeply indebted for typing the script, particularly for deciphering my illegible handwriting of what was, to her, a largely unfamiliar vocabulary. My debt to Coventry City Libraries is manifold; the Department has provided me with all the matter on which I have written but, more than that, it gave me the privilege of working for nearly twenty years in a job of constantly changing but unfailing interest.

ALICE LYNES

August 1973

Chapter 1
The Function of the Local Collection

THE changes that have taken place in the post-war years in the approach to the study of history have opened up fields of enquiry to increasing numbers of would-be students. New methods and materials of research and an emphasis on local studies, both in relation to and distinct from national history, have brought the subject within the range of the layman. The changing landscape and pattern of society, the evidences of the past revealed by wartime destruction and the opportunities presented for investigation in the course of redevelopment, have contributed to a widespread interest in local studies. Stimulated by television programmes on archaeology, history and our architectural heritage and increasing facilities for exploring the past, by visiting the great houses and other historic monuments, many are taking a closer look at familiar things about them and speculating on the past. Satisfying this enquiry presents to public libraries both a challenge and an opportunity. The local library is the only place in the area, with the exceptions to be discussed in Chapter 4, where the increasingly wide variety of material needed for local studies can be collected and made available for use. The function of the library is to provide for the reading requirements, in the broadest sense, of all members of the community and, if it is fulfilling that function, it is to the library that all enquirers, including newcomers to the field, will naturally turn.

Most public libraries have local collections; some of these, in large cities, are of long standing and are very extensive. Others, including some small libraries, collect manuscript records and number archivists among their staff; some confine their collecting to secondary source material. In many places the local collection consists of a small section in the reference library, in others, although more extensive, the stock comprises an unorganized accumulation awaiting the time when staff and funds can be provided to catalogue it and make it workable to full capacity. Some potentially fine collections have suffered from being the sole responsibility of a member of the staff, perhaps the librarian himself, who has grown up with the collection and over a long period been its 'catalogue'. This, perhaps, sufficed when the use of the collection was limited to a few scholars and antiquarians but, when he was no longer there to guide the enquirer along its byways, it was left completely unsuited to meet the demands put upon it in recent years. Many collections grew up haphazardly, as gifts were offered and opportunities arose to acquire material, with little thought for planning and with the almost total exclusion of the contemporary material which the historian of today finds lacking. Standards of accommodation and staffing are as variable as the collections. An increasing number are housed in separate rooms to which the public have access; some planned for the purpose, well equipped and with trained staff qualified to carry out the specialist duties required. Others are in separate rooms used for some other purpose and only privileged readers are admitted. Most librarians are fully conscious of their responsibility to develop the local collection and where they have been given the opportunity to do this the library's prestige within the community has been enhanced. As service improves, the demand increases and what, in some quarters, may have been considered an extravagance has soon proved to be worthwhile.

There is, perhaps, too great a tendency to refer to the local collection as the Local History Department; those libraries which have adopted the name Department of Local Studies have recognized the wider field over which their endeavours must range if they are to serve their true purpose. Every member of the community has a right to the use of his public library and, as in the other departments this is being acknowledged by the provision for others than readers of books, so provision should be made in the local collection for those who are concerned with other aspects of the locality than its history. Perhaps, too, 'local study' is not wholly apposite, for much of the work of the department is concerned with providing local information of the quick reference type. Some places have established information centres either within the library or elsewhere; where this has not been done, the local collection must assume the responsibility.

To meet the requirements of all its readers the local collection must have two principal objectives; to collect and organize, in such a way that it will be readily available for use, anything which contributes to a knowledge of the area in the past and also that which is news today and will be source material for the history of our time in the future. The first presents no great difficulty, for it can easily be ascertained whether an item adds to what is already in the collection. Current material does present problems; except, perhaps, in the limited field of a special collection, it is impossible to collect everything. Selection must be made; some guidance in assessing the possible value of material for future use may be had from the relative importance of the matter it concerns in local affairs of the present time. Historians will want to know what impact burning questions of today had on the area, and librarians must ensure that material is preserved that will tell them. Profit may also be made from the frustration often experienced due to the lack of some information not having been handed down, by making certain that the omission is not repeated.

Of all readers making use of the local collection, those engaged in education, either as teacher or student from university down to primary school level, are in the majority. Where the library has no archive collection, work at university level will be confined largely to undergraduates preparing theses for degrees. They may be students from a local university but, more often, they are local residents studying away from home who have chosen to write on a local subject, working intensively during vacations. Their work on material in the library will usually be complementary to work on documents in the local record office, and they will generally have discussed the available sources with the librarian of the local collection and the archivist before choosing a subject. Difficulty arises when a non-local student at a distant university writes announcing the intention of writing a thesis on a local subject which may have become national news, such as the redevelopment of bomb-damaged Coventry. Much of the source material cannot be lent for use in the student's local library; the cost of photocopying it would be prohibitive and the student is unable or unwilling to travel to the library to use it. Commonsense often prevails in the alternative choice of a subject. During recent years the university extra-mural departments have been doing much to promote local studies by organizing group work among members of the general public. This is usually based on the examination and transcription of local records and may concern, for example, some aspect of village history or a town street at a particular period. The local collection can serve a useful purpose in this work by providing students with material for a general background knowledge of the area they are studying, without which much of their work lacks meaning. And in places with no record office, a meeting place can sometimes be provided for a group, by arranging for documents in private or public ownership to be deposited temporarily for work under the guidance of the tutor. Apart from the personal satisfaction such students derive, their work often produces a useful publication.

Colleges of education, polytechnics, colleges of art and technology and colleges of further education provide the local collection with many of its readers. Students frequently choose subjects of local interest, having some relation to their course of study, for extended essays or theses to be submitted for a diploma or degree. The teaching of history in schools is emphasizing the need for a child to identify himself with his environment, by linking local events to the course of national history, and local studies occupy a prominent place in college of education courses. Students, during their teaching practice, should be able to find in the local collection information on local aspects of the subjects they teach to introduce into the lessons they are preparing. The value of local studies is also recognized by colleges of art where students are encouraged to use the library's local collection to study something of the history of the local buildings they draw. In places where there is an active theatre, this sometimes assumes a teaching role. A team of teacher-actors produce plays on historical topics, often from a local aspect, which are performed as lessons in the local schools. One such Theatre in Education has gathered much of its material from the library's local collection.

Local studies have a prominent place in the individual work which children in, principally, comprehensive and secondary modern schools are encouraged to do. With co-operation between the teacher and librarian, working sessions in the library during school hours can produce good results. Given due notice, it should be possible to produce material from which even the child who is not very bright can extract some information to give him a sense of achievement. Side-tracking sometimes occurs when a child discovers, perhaps, his father's name in the local directory, but exploration among books is something not to be discouraged. Investigations into local heraldry are often made to produce a badge for a new school, or into the lives of benefactors whose interest was in education, or other celebrities to provide names for schools with a house system. There is a growing tendency to assign 'projects' in local history to very young children in primary schools. Producing material within their capability of understanding is very difficult; they can only be 'spoon-fed' with the simplest that can be found, but if they can be sent away satisfied with their 'research', they are potential readers.

Much of the work of the local collection is in answering the questions that arise in the course of everyday business in all spheres of public life. Some typical examples from one library show how widely these can range. The defence in a case brought for car parking was made on the grounds that no offence took place in the street named. Old maps, a photograph of another street showing a nameplate of the street cited and other evidence from the local collection were produced in court and the case was dismissed. For a period, the librarian of the local collection was responsible for suggesting names having local significance for streets on new housing estates, and breweries enlist assistance in choosing suitable local names for new public houses. The restorers of a fine Tudor almshouse, destroyed during the last war, were able to use photographs, drawings and plans from the library's collection. An artist, commissioned to produce a mural for a large supermarket, based his design on a large-scale map hanging on the wall in the department, and a firm of interior decorators used old prints to produce enlarged photographic murals. Material in the department has been used in the production of television programmes. A list of local places associated with historic events or celebrities was compiled for the preparation of commemorative plaques. The press, public departments, commerce and industry are among those who should be able to expect the local collection to provide them with the information they require on any matter of local interest.

'Local historian' is a name sometimes assumed by, but more often assigned by others to, those who have little claim to it. The professional local historian is inclined to scorn or patronize the amateur as a compiler of facts relating to his immediate locality, rather than an interpreter of the records he meticulously copies. He is, more correctly, an antiquarian pursuing a course satisfying to himself and to many who are like-minded and his efforts require equal attention to that afforded the professional. Much of the material used by the professional historian will be found in the national libraries and record repositories and in local record offices but, depending upon his subject, the local collection is likely to include material for his purpose. Newspapers particularly, are an acknowledged primary source of contemporary history and the collection which includes files of the local newspapers has much to offer. A writer commissioned to produce a business history often finds himself in the unenviable position of having no records to work on, business concerns being notoriously ruthless in destroying anything unconnected with their present activities and plans for the future. The local collection can often produce newscuttings, brochures and printed reports to supply him with some information.

For the amateur the study of local history provides something of the excitement of detective work, relaxation from the pressures of daily life and, often, a new interest on reaching retirement. Interests range widely. A doctor, arranging a small exhibition in connection with the opening of a new medical institution, becomes absorbed in the activities of his predecessors; a painter of watercolours spends years in collecting information about the buildings he has painted, or a schoolmaster finds a new occupation in unravelling the history of the village to which he has retired. Some amateur historians may be working in a professional capacity. Anticipating the merger of the local police force, an officer compiles its history; a post office worker is able to collect, from unexpected sources, a great deal of information about the postal services of the area, and fire officers find in the local collection material to supplement their own records for the production of a brochure marking the centenary of the fire brigade. Whatever his interest or ability, the amateur historian should find in the local collection something for his purpose and assistance in using it.

Of recent years preoccupation with the past has extended rapidly to remote times. Developments of scientific methods of archaeological investigation, the popularity of radio and television programmes and lectures on the subject, and the opportunity to watch work being carried out by the professional archaeologists who, in growing numbers, are being appointed to the staff of local authorities and development corporations, are providing a new interest to many. The library can play its part by collecting material for the use of archaeologists of all grades and also to provide a record, for future reference, of discoveries made. The active archaeologist, professional or amateur, needs to have as complete a knowledge as possible of what has occupied the site he is about to excavate. Maps, old prints, accounts of ancient buildings and reports of earlier finds will assist in his preparatory work. A good deal of work was done by competent archaeologists during building activity in many towns in Victorian times. Although their conclusions may not now be acceptable, the reports and plans they made can be useful. For the 'armchair' or 'peephole' archaeologist and for future record, all available reports of local excavations should be collected from local and national journals, archaeological societies' transactions and, often, the newsletter produced by the local archaeological research group to be found in many places. Close touch kept with local archaeological work can be mutually advantageous. Much recording is either never published or delayed; it may be possible to borrow notes, plans and drawings for copying, or to obtain prints from photographs taken. The librarian can sometimes help the archaeologist in recruiting practical assistance. He meets many would-be excavators of all ages; these he can put in touch with local groups and he can also try to impress upon the enquirer the irremediable damage that can be done by the enthusiastic but untrained digger.

Enquiry into family history and the tracing of ancestors is an engrossing occupation for many, and the local collection will frequently be called upon to assist enquirers, both in person and by letter, often from the United States and the Commonwealth. The latter sometimes expect a family tree to be gratuitously provided; it is no function of the library to do enquirers' research but, if staffing permits, a limited amount of checking for specific enquiries might be made, and the name and address of a professional record searcher supplied from the list prepared by the Society of Local Archivists which should always be available. For the personal enquirer the local collection should be able to provide some material, such as directories, poll books, obituary notices and biographical information, often to be found among newscuttings and in scrapbooks. The Census *Enumerators' Books* for 1841 to 1881, obtainable on microfilm from the Public Record Office, are a valuable source of information to the genealogist while in some areas many parish registers have been published. Information on the parish registers available at the Society of Genealogists, the whereabouts of wills, any records in the local record office (such as apprenticeship rolls), and on registrations of births, marriages and deaths since 1837 at the General Register Office at Somerset House should be available to direct enquirers' further searches.

Apart from these categories of reader, the local collection should provide for the multiplicity of enquiries by the general public. These may include the height above sea level of some point, the parish to which a particular house is attached, a blacksmith who will make a wrought-iron gate, when a famous actor played at the local theatre or the name of the architect of a local building. Addresses are constantly required, frequently by postal enquiry, and the ability to trace these depends on the availability of up-to-date directories. Amateur artists wanting to paint historic buildings copy the collection's illustrations; the purchaser of an old house wants to know its history and a visitor to the district wants to know what houses are open to the public and when. Small study groups of Townswomen's Guilds and Women's Institutes often choose topics of local interest and work individually or as a group on material in the collection; and many a bet would appear to be settled, by reference to old directories, as to what trader occupied certain premises at a particular date. Among the general public who also frequent the local collection are those with no special interest beyond a love of their native place; to them the collection affords the opportunity for pleasant browsing.

The wide variety of members of the community and their requirements of the local collection have been detailed, but how far does that community extend? The area to be covered should be defined at the outset and the material collected limited to that area. It may be a town, confined to its boundaries or including neighbouring places coming within its sphere of influence, or it may cover the county. Regard must be taken of other libraries in the area, with their local and special collections.

Coventry's collection, started long before the County Library was established, covers also the county of Warwick. Material on Coventry is collected intensively but only very general material of a limited amount is included about Birmingham, Leamington, Nuneaton, Rugby, Stratford-upon-Avon and Warwick, whose libraries have their own local collections. The county's greatest local author receives little attention; with Birmingham's Shakespeare Memorial Library and the Shakespeare Centre at Stratford-upon-Avon, collecting Shakespeariana would be futile. Competitive collection of rare material should be avoided and can be by co-operation between neighbouring libraries. If each library, to the best of its resources, builds up its collection to cover its own area, the needs of the public in the field of local study will be well served.

Chapter 2
Fields of Local Study

IT HAS already been said that it is the function of the local collection to endeavour to meet the requirements of all members of the community in their quest for information on every aspect of life in the area covered by the collection. In effect, the local collection should aim to provide in a specialized way as wide a subject coverage as does the general library. The fields of knowledge covered by the systems librarians have devised for arranging the media of communication they have assembled, in a manner best suited for convenient use by themselves and the public, are almost all applicable to the study of a locality and should be represented in the collection. The *Dewey Decimal Classification* provides a convenient framework for a statement of what those fields are, together with some examples of the available material which might be included and the queries it might be used to answer.

GENERALITIES

No library can hope to possess all the material relevant to the study of its locality, but the librarian of the local collection will be better equipped to satisfy readers' requirements if the collection includes material giving information on the existence and possible location of anything relating to the subject of the enquiry. There exist for many areas bibliographies and checklists which may be a useful tool for the librarian in his continuing search for additions to the collection but, even if the items listed are unobtainable, the fact that they exist can be made known to the enquirer, giving the alternatives of possibly borrowing them or obtaining photocopies or using them in the library possessing them. Such bibliographies may vary in size from the *Regional Lists* reprinted from the Library Association's *British Humanities Index* to Thomas Chubb's *The Printed Maps in the Atlases of Great Britain and Ireland*. They include handlists produced by antiquaries and antiquarian booksellers, bibliographies of local authors published, perhaps, on such an occasion as a centenary, and catalogues of special collections in public or private ownership. As an example, Thomas Sharp, an eighteenth/nineteenth-century Coventry antiquary, commissioned a local drawing-master to make some seven hundred drawings of churches, mansions and other buildings to illustrate his copy of Dr Thomas's enlarged edition of *Dugdale's Antiquities of Warwickshire*. The collection was later sold to the Earl of Aylesford, by whose name it is now known, and eventually acquired by the Birmingham Reference Library. Some of the drawings are of buildings—many no longer standing—in Coventry and its vicinity and a list of these, supplied by Birmingham, has been much used by the staff of Coventry's local collection in obtaining photocopies of some, or in directing enquirers to Birmingham to use the originals. It is not suggested that copies of all such bibliographies should be on stock in the local collection; the place for Chubb's *Maps*, for example, is the general reference library and if the local collection is adjacent to or a part of this, it is readily available and there should be no question of duplicating it. It should, nevertheless, be regarded as essential to the local collection and either included in an index to material located elsewhere or, in some cases, a copy of the relevant sections could be made for use in the collection.

The works of local authors will have their place in every local collection. Many of these are on some topic of local interest and will be included for their subject content, but others will be collected solely on grounds of authorship. The definition of a local author is a matter on which opinion is divided; some libraries 'claim' an author on the grounds of his having been born in the place; others by virtue of his working life having been spent there. The latter would appear to be the more reasonable. Local pride should be subordinated to a common-sense attitude to the matter, calling for agreement on policy between rival 'claimants'. What is important is to ensure that an author's works are collected somewhere and this should be done with the avoidance of wasted resources and effort. Local authors are not limited to the field of imaginative writing; they may be scientists, architects, photographers, town-planners. Some may have their works included in the local collection although they spent only a comparatively short time in the area. For example, a textbook on biology, based on classwork done by the author with the sixth form of a local school, would have a legitimate place as the work of a local author, but would also provide, in the future, material for a history of teaching methods.

Library science is an obvious subject for inclusion in every local collection. Profiting by the knowledge that many organizations and institutions find, at some stage, a need for records that have been destroyed, it can be ensured that the librarian's successors shall have no cause for reproaching him in this respect. Annual reports, printed catalogues and booklists, brochures issued in connection with openings of new libraries or inaugurating new services and copies of all other publications should be preserved. Files of press-cuttings should also be maintained together with any papers on professional subjects read by the librarian or members of the staff. Even where there is a local record office, it would be an advantage for the library to preserve its own archives. When these cease to be in current use for administrative purposes, those considered worth permanent preservation should be passed to the local collection. Apart from being the raw material of the library's history, much of this can be of practical administrative value. For example, one library established in the last quarter of the nineteenth century had received numerous cash bequests. A tally of these was made from old reports and arrangements made with the authority's Treasurer to set up a bequest fund, from which special purchases can be made without drawing on the annual book fund. Many places had some library provision before the advent of local authority libraries; in some cases they were absorbed in the public library when this was established. They include school libraries, parish libraries, Mechanics' Institute libraries and subscription libraries, sometimes attached to a learned society. Material relating to these and to any other libraries within the area should be collected.

Periodical publications account for a considerable part of the stock of most local collections, but the majority of them are concerned with one particular subject and so are excluded from those under present consideration. In any community there are always people with an urge to air their views on a variety of matters and these often produce a magazine. Many are short-lived and may be considered trifling, but they often include information not to be found elsewhere and should be given serious consideration, both for collecting current issues and searching out obsolete publications.

Local newspapers are one of the most valuable sources of information on almost every aspect of the life of a community. Political bias may often colour reports but the practised reader will learn to be discriminating. Libraries possessing files of early newspapers are fortunate indeed, but none should fail to collect current issues, for they frequently provide the only information there is on some particular topic. More is said about the place of newspapers in the local collection in a later chapter.

It is usual to include books printed in the locality although not after, maybe, 1850 or some other accepted date. For the purpose of the local collection such books may be considered as rarities, of which there will probably be a wide variety. It would be impossible and pointless to collect everything printed locally in modern times, although there may be important exceptions to the general dateline. One instance of this is at Coventry. There, one firm installed one of the earliest four-colour-printing machines to be used in this country, to enable them to print catalogues for the motor trade, with cars in their true colours.

Some examples of books they produced on these machines, profusely illustrated in the style of illuminated manuscripts, are included in the collection. Other exceptions may be the productions of the great private presses, such as Hammersmith's Kelmscott Press collection. Books formerly in the possession of some prominent local person or institution have their place, and may be of particular interest if they have been 'defaced' by annotations. Some years ago Coventry was able to purchase for a nominal sum a few volumes from the Grammar School Library, established in 1602, and in some quarters said to be the first public library in the country. After being shamefully misused the remnants were dispersed in the early years of this century. Several of the books were printed before 1500 and one is inscribed with the names of several scholars, some of them men who later made their mark in various spheres of public life. Examples of the work of outstanding local bookbinders should also be included, with any distinctive styles such as 'Dutch' boards or 'cottage' style.

PHILOSOPHY

The Philosophy class is unlikely to be represented in all collections, but in some places there will be societies for the study of philosophical subjects, whose activities and, possibly, publications will provide material which should be included. In some rural areas, a lively interest in the tradition of witchcraft has produced a considerable amount of writing, which can be valuable to anyone studying the subject. Many places have their ghost stories; interest in these is revived from time to time and the local collection will preserve any evidence there is on the subject.

RELIGION

Material relating to all aspects of the religious life of the area, past and present, will be included in the collection. In many places, in addition to Anglican, Roman Catholic and Non-Conformist denominational churches, there are immigrant populations who have established places of worship for non-Christian religions, such as Mohammedanism, Hinduism and Buddhism. Consecrations, installations of clergy, services for special occasions, such as important national or local events, will produce orders of service and other material for the collection. Some cathedrals and churches have their own forms of service or specially composed hymns; these, if available in published form, should be included. The salaries of Church of England clergy were in some areas paid by a specially authorized local rate, the levying of which was fiercely contested by Non-Conformists. Reports of demonstrations and published protests throw light on the subject of church finance and, often, on the people involved. Sermons, including funeral orations and episcopal charges, frequently published until the present century, provide useful information on questions of the day and on the lives of prominent local people. The work of the churches in the field of social service will be recorded in reports by associations connected with the church, such as the YMCA. These should be collected together with programmes and any other publications connected with missions and religious conferences held in the area. Many of our towns developed around a monastic house which was established in the Middle Ages and continued to exert an important influence on the district until the Dissolution. Any material relating to these establishments, as also to any houses founded in more recent times, will have its place in the collection. The lives of saints associated with the area and records of religious persecutions that may have taken place should also be included.

SOCIAL SCIENCES

The subjects covered by the Social Sciences class will probably account for a considerable proportion of the local collection's stock, embracing as it does so many aspects of community life. The complexities of modern living are increasingly exercising the attention of social scientists and planners, and groups in many universities and colleges have carried out sociological surveys in their area. These often include information not available elsewhere and can provide valuable material for a variety of the library's users. Some have been published, perhaps in stencilled form; in other cases it may be possible, with the co-operation of the group concerned, to obtain a typescript.

Census reports, published county by county, provide statistics of the population of administrative areas essential to workers in many fields. Reports from 1801–51 covering wider areas were published in 1852, giving only numbers of inhabitants, with numbers of houses for places with a population of more than 2,000. Since that date tables have been added giving populations under such groups as age, marital conditions, occupation, birthplace, infirmity and education. Preliminary reports are published soon after the Census is taken, but the delay in the appearance of the full reports tends to devalue the wealth of additional analyses of the social pattern included in those of more recent date. As a result of the accelerating rate of social change, the latest available statistics can often be misleading; the report of the intercensal 10 per cent sample Census of 1966 for places of over 15,000 population is particularly useful for this reason. The Occupational Tables provide a wealth of information for the social and industrial historian, but since the statistics for the nineteenth century were on a county basis, their value for comparative purposes is limited.

The relations of individuals and groups within the community may have far-reaching effects on the social and economic development of the area. Material on the subject will probably consist largely of newspaper reports, but there may be propaganda material issued by the groups or reports by public departments concerned with them. The rights and duties of citizenship will be covered by the publications of citizens' guilds which exist in many places and by material on the freedom granted in some old towns, from medieval times.

Parliamentary representation has produced records which can be of value for purposes other than that for which they were intended. Poll books and more recent registers of electors list, with the extension of the franchise, an increasing proportion of a place's inhabitants and can often provide a substitute for directories where none exist for the period. Candidates' speeches and records of elections can throw light on the social and economic conditions as well as the political climate of the time. The activities of political parties will be recorded in reports of meetings, speeches, manifestos and a variety of other publications.

Since the last war many towns have become 'twinned' with places abroad, with exchange of visits and loan exhibitions and, sometimes, gifts of material illustrating the life and culture of each. Libraries can play an important part in fostering such links and the local collection would seem to be the appropriate department for assembling and housing such exhibitions and gifts.

The economic affairs of a place will include the organization of labour, working conditions, living standards, wages and strikes, matters not only for historians of the past and the future, but for many organizations concerned with the day-to-day running of affairs.

Finance will be covered by such records as medieval subsidy rolls and poll tax returns and by reports of local banks, stock exchanges and similar institutions. The land and its ownership, both private and corporate, and the use made of it is dealt with in books ranging from *Domesday Book*, of which the appropriate sections are included in the *Victoria County Histories*, to the *Land Utilisation Surveys*. Co-operative economic effort should be represented in the collection by the reports of such bodies as building societies, co-operative production and consumer societies and friendly societies. Material on production and economic organization may extend from the medieval craft guilds to the current productivity exercises of some local industrial concern.

Law and its administration will have its place in the local

collection with reports of civil and criminal trials, accounts of the work of the courts, and statutes relating to local matters.

Changes in the administration of the area may be recorded in a succession of publications ranging from early council books or town clerks' journals, which have been printed for some places, through the reports of the municipal commissioners leading to the Municipal Corporations Act of 1836 and official handbooks issued by the local authority to the reorganization of local government now about to be put into effect. The growth of public services may be traced in the files of annual or other reports of local government departments and from programmes issued for the ceremonial opening of new buildings or services, often giving plans and illustrations and other useful data. There may be training establishments in the area for the armed forces, or a county regiment may have its headquarters there. Units may have been stationed during the last two wars and in many places there will have been some organization for the mobilization of defence from early times. Regimental magazines and histories, accounts of actions in which local units took part, together with accounts of battles fought in the area, are among material on military history.

The associations and institutions which are the centre of community life will provide much material. Before the state assumed many of its present responsibilities, the provisions of many services and institutions were dependent upon the benevolence of the wealthier members of the community. Most places, large and small, have enjoyed charitable bequests for several centuries. The early nineteenth-century reports of the charity commissioners, together with later schemes made to adapt the use of funds for modern requirements, provide valuable information on the early history of many institutions such as schools, hospitals and almshouses. Hospitals, prisons and reformatories issue reports and are reported on; societies such as Freemasons produce histories and some social societies, such as Rotary, may publish magazines. These are all the material of social history.

Educational activity at all levels and in all fields whether by the local authority or independent bodies, will be covered by publications including prospectuses, handbooks, students' magazines, programmes of 'open days' and 'education weeks', prize-givings and graduation ceremonies. The published minutes of the local education authority provide information on administration as do charity commissioners' schemes for endowed schools. Pioneer work carried out locally, such as the comprehensive system, will be the subject of articles in educational journals and papers read to professional associations.

The widespread and growing interest in transport history and the increasing volume of traffic of all kinds is both producing material on the subject and making it essential to collect everything that becomes available on transportation in the area, whether it be by road, railway, sea or inland waterway or air. This includes roadbooks, time and fare tables and shipping information (often given in local newspapers), maps, articles in journals, transportation surveys, reports on projected roads, car parking and all other related matters. Closely linked with transport facilities is commercial prosperity. Chamber of Commerce reports, surveys on shopping by the local authority planning department, anniversary publications of stores and other business houses, are among items to be collected on the subject.

The observance of ancient customs, the wearing of special regional dress or that of local trade and other once-common practices are fast dying out, but the local collection can ensure that they do not pass out of knowledge by preserving any relevant material, written or pictorial, both relating to the past and to any customs and folklore practices that may have survived, such as processions, mummers' plays, or ceremonies peculiar to the area. Some legends have produced an extensive literature, as Lady Godiva at Coventry. In some places chapbooks have survived in considerable numbers. Population movement and the mass-communication agencies are obliterating the local dialects which were a distinguishing characteristic of regional life. Dialect dictionaries have been published for many areas; some places, such as the Black Country, have produced monologues and other dialect literature. These, together with any vocal or phonetic records if possible, should be preserved.

PURE SCIENCES

Most branches of science come within the scope of the local collection. Scientific societies may publish reports and proceedings of their meetings; adult education organizations, such as the Workers' Educational Association, run lectures on scientific subjects as did the Mechanics' Institutes of the nineteenth century. Programmes and reports of these together with syllabuses and publications of any institutions for the full-time study of science are all potentially useful. If there is an observatory in the area, there will probably also be an astronomical society; any reports they may produce should be acquired. The geological structure, water supply and atmospheric conditions of an area are largely responsible for the course of its development. Geological maps, *Memoirs of the Geological Survey* and meteorological reports will be included in this section. The Ordnance Survey *Soil Surveys* and the large-scale coal-seam maps published by the National Coal Board Scientific Department are material for the economic geologist. Plant and animal life of the present and prehistoric times will be recorded in the proceedings of societies for the study of botany, zoology and palaeontology, in observations recorded at nature reserves and bird sanctuaries and in guidebooks to botanical and zoological gardens and arboreta. Coventry has a collection of drawings made in the nineteenth century of ancient Warwickshire oaks, with details of measurements and notes on their history.

TECHNOLOGY

The applied sciences provide a wide scope for local studies, both from the standpoint of history and enquiry on current matters.

Subject coverage will vary probably more than in any other section of the local collection, dependent upon the character of the place. An industrial area will include little, if anything, on agriculture, or a rural area on engineering, chemical technology or manufactures. An academic or tourist centre will probably include none of these. In an industrial area serial publications, or articles from them, on matters of general or specific technological interest to the locality, should be filed. Material relating to the activities of societies and institutions, including colleges or other agencies for the teaching of technology, should also be collected. Specifications of patents for local products or processes, or by local inventors, are of current and historical interest.

The medical sciences will have a place in all local collections. By-laws and regulations relating to public health, publicity material and reports of exhibitions and other work directed to health education together with the annual reports of the chief medical officer and, sometimes, his heads of department, are a contribution to social as well as medical history. Local executive councils of the National Health Service produce lists of practitioners in all branches of medicine, with details of the service provided. A selection of these might be usefully retained for historic record after they cease to supply current information. Reports of local innovations in medical practice with details and, possibly, illustrations of apparatus, are sources of general as well as local medical history.

The local collection should collect everything available on any staple industry of the locality, such as some branch of engineering, a chemical, manufacturing or assembling industry. Catalogues of products and other publicity material, journals and histories produced by the firms involved, press reports of shareholders' meetings and other matters concerning them, and periodical articles and books which have a bearing on the industry as carried on locally, are all relevant. Libraries in coastal areas will probably have material on naval installations, and many old towns on their walls and other means of defence. Projects for the construction of roads, waterworks, sewage and refuse disposal and other such works will produce reports and plans and often be the subject of a public enquiry. The problem of air pollution is claiming attention everywhere; smokeless zones are being declared. The local collection should preserve a record of all such projects. Railway history has many followers. In many places disused light railways are a relic of some now-forgotten industry; in others, enthusiasts maintain a model railway. Maps and photographs are among the sources of information to be kept.

In a county area, particularly one which is predominantly rural, the local collection will give emphasis to agricultural activities. Organizations concerned with various types of farming will have their local branches; there may be research stations and farming schools. Reports will be published and meetings reported. Specialists in some branch of agriculture may contribute articles to farming journals. Contests and shows are an important part of the life of an agricultural community; catalogues provide a record of contemporary practice.

The domestic arts are, probably, somewhat neglected as a subject for inclusion in the local collection. Some places have traditional dishes, sometimes eaten at a particular season; many more have become a memory. In some quarters there is a revival of interest in such cookery and efforts to collect recipes would be worthwhile. Recording the present as history for the future might well be applied to the domestic scene. Pictorial records of typical homes could usefully be added to the collection. High in the domestic arts of England is the art of innkeeping. Most collections will have material on the old inns of the area, as also on some modern ones.

In the business field, the area may have been or may still be an important centre of printing and publishing. The collection should include material on the firms and people concerned. Printers' trade cards, exhibiting their variety of types, throw a fascinating light on the history of printing.

Extensive building operations in the post-war era have produced new constructional methods. Some of these, pioneered by local authorities, have been much publicized in building trade journals and elsewhere. Descriptive material should be added to the collection, together with information on early methods of building construction, often revealed during the demolition of old buildings in the course of redevelopment.

THE ARTS

Most libraries will have the opportunity of including in their local collection materials ranging over much of the arts field. The activities of arts societies, schools of art, and art galleries and museums, will be recorded in such items as programmes of meetings, prospectuses, reviews and catalogues of exhibitions, monographs on special exhibits, details of important purchases, donations and bequests.

Environmental planning has gathered impetus since the last war. Local authorities are developing new areas, redeveloping to meet the demands of modern living and, in some places, carrying out the renewal of run-down areas or creating conservation areas. Controlling legislation requires the submission of plans and the holding of public enquiries. Publicity regarding these together with published plans and any material relating to parks, cemeteries, open spaces, etc., should be collected.

The architectural section will cover all the important buildings of the locality, ancient and modern. Public buildings may include town halls and central and local government buildings, banks, law courts, market halls, shops, railway stations, hospitals, theatres. Buildings for religious purposes could range from ruins of a medieval monastery to the church built in a newly created city parish. Schools, colleges and universities and dwellings of all types from castles to country cottages, complete the range of architectural styles on which information may be gathered from such sources as architectural publications, papers read to archaeological or civic societies and estate agents' publicity.

Students of sculpture may find local examples in monumental effigies in cathedral or church, statues in public buildings or on outdoor sites and the work of modern artists introduced into the landscaping of new areas. Stone- and wood-carvings decorate the exterior and interior of religious and secular buildings old and new. In medieval times coins of the realm were minted in a number of provincial towns and during the sixteenth, seventeenth and eighteenth centuries, token coins were struck for use when small change was in short supply. These attract keen collectors and finds produce frequent enquiries. Among examples of ceramic art are mosaics in areas where there are Roman sites, and decorated tiles found *in situ* on floors and walls of old buildings or in medieval tile kilns during archaeological digs. The metalworker's art may include screens, lecterns, pulpits and other fittings in churches, church and, perhaps, civic plate, park gates and bronze doors to important buildings. The collection should be able to produce information on all these subjects.

In places where there is an art gallery, the local collection is unlikely to collect drawings of artistic value, but will confine itself to those of topographical or other purely local interest. It should, however, collect any material available about the artists. In rural areas, particularly, traditional crafts were, and sometimes still are, practised. Information on design, methods of working, material used and the people concerned should be collected if possible. Some places may have been centres of tapestry weaving, such as Barcheston of Sheldon tapestry fame, or may possess tapestries widely known, such as that in Coventry's Guildhall of St Mary and Graham Sutherland's in the cathedral there. Pictorial records, descriptive literature, historic references and published evaluations, should be preserved.

Many places are rich in stained glass, both medieval and modern. Much of it has been closely studied and widely written about in the journals of learned societies and elsewhere. This should all be available for the enquirer.

As with drawings, the collection of paintings and prints as art forms will be the province of the art gallery, but any material on

2

local schools of painting or the work of individual artists will have its place in the local collection, as will prints of topographical interest. A recent development of print-making is the growing practice of issuing first-day cover envelopes to mark special occasions, such as the Shakespeare Quatercentenary at Stratford-upon-Avon and the centenary of the bicycle at Coventry. These should be added to other souvenirs of the occasion.

Musical activities may range widely to cover all aspects of music and music making in the area. These will include performances of choral, operatic and orchestral societies, visiting artists or combinations and musical festivals. Formal musical education may be provided in schools of music, institutions for further education and schools; programmes, reports and syllabuses of all these should be collected. The area may have produced or become the home of some outstanding musician or a work may have been composed for or first performed at a local event such as Britten's *War Requiem* for the festival celebrating the consecration of Coventry Cathedral. The scores of such compositions, together with any other local music such as regimental marches, traditional songs, dance tunes or carols, would have their place in the collection. So, too, would any recordings made by local artists, orchestras and choirs, or performances on some famous instrument, such as an organ, which may be located in the area.

Most places will have associations and institutions for the promotion of recreation. The theatre may have continued to occupy an important place in community life over a long period; playbills, programmes, criticisms, drawings and, of more recent times, photographs of stage design and costumes, of both the professional and amateur theatre, provide material for the student or historian.

Competitive events connected with indoor and outdoor sports and amusements, ranging from bridge to wrestling and from cricket to walking, together with regattas, air pageants and horse-race meetings, may produce programmes, reports and pictorial records for preservation. Collection should also be made of any material relating to sports and pastimes of the past which may have been peculiar to the locality and, in some places, still survive.

LITERATURE

Some libraries may be able to include a considerable amount of imaginative literature depicting the locality in the form of poetry, drama, novels or essays. Writing may be descriptive, such as Richard Jago's poem *Edgehill*, 'delineating' the towns and villages of Warwickshire, or they may reflect local life at some period, as *Middlemarch* does early nineteenth-century Coventry, and *Tom Brown's Schooldays* life at Rugby School. They may be based on historical fact, as Scott's *Kenilworth*, on the biography of a local celebrity, as Brophy's *Gentleman of Stratford*, or use the area as a setting, as Mrs Braddon's *The Doctor's Wife* does Coventry. Some places, such as York and Coventry, were famous for their medieval miracle plays. Surviving texts, together with modern adaptations and works of criticism, should be collected.

GEOGRAPHY AND HISTORY

Although most of the foregoing topics, as applied to a locality, may be considered 'history', there still remains much which will have its place in the local collection under that heading. Much of the published writing on local matters is of a miscellaneous nature, which can only be classified under the general term 'history'. Local history societies flourish in many places; papers read at meetings or published in their journals often represent important pieces of historical research and can be valuable additions to the library's stock. Not only is it the function of the local collection to provide the material for studying the locality, but, as will be enlarged upon in Chapter 9, the librarian is frequently required to act as teacher in the methods of historical study. Of recent years a number of excellent books and pamphlets on the subject have been published while the *Local Historian*, formerly the *Amateur Historian*, continues to provide helpful articles on material and methods of history in its broadest sense. These are essential tools for the librarian and reader and should be in every local collection.

The study of the geography of an area is essential to an understanding of its development. Among material on the subject are guidebooks, often including accounts of travels in the area in the seventeenth and eighteenth centuries, directories, maps, pictorial records, place-name studies and reports of archaeological research. Early nineteenth-century guidebooks were frequently little masterpieces, mines of information, often illustrated by rare prints. They can be a valuable asset to the collection, as can also directories, although not all places are fortunate enough to have been well catered for in this respect.

In the study of a locality, the people who have shaped its course figure prominently. The giants will be the subject of full-scale biographies, which should be relatively easy to obtain, but the lesser lights are more elusive. Scraps of information will need to be gathered from any available source, such as obituary notices, biographical dictionaries and newspaper reports. Autobiographies and diaries, often modest little publications privately printed, are worth searching for, not only for biographical details but for the light they throw on the local life of their time. Genealogical investigation is of absorbing interest to many and, although the library which is not also a record repository will not hold the essential records for research, there should be material to give some pointers to the enquirer, such as directories, poll books, Census returns and obituary notices and, in some places, collections of transcripts of tombstone inscriptions. The landowning families of the area will probably be the subject of family histories or published genealogical tables. Where this is not so, copies of *Burke's Peerage* and *Landed Gentry* might be transferred from the reference library when they are replaced by new editions, or photocopies made of the relevant sections. Heraldry, 'the shorthand of history', has a wide following. The *Heraldic Visitations* of the area, giving genealogical tables and coats-of-arms, together with any later material, such as details of grants of arms to local families or public bodies, or guides to the heraldic decoration on some public building, should have their place in the collection.

Histories of the area may range from scholarly works to short articles in a parish magazine by a local amateur and may include some of the excellent short village histories being produced by groups of local history researchers, often working under the guidance of extra-mural departments of the universities. Works may cover the history of the area from its beginning or may be confined to a limited period or some particular event, or some work not specifically on the area may be added to the collection for the relevant information it may contain.

SPECIAL COLLECTIONS

Many libraries have special collections on some topic of local interest. This may be the library of some eminent local person; it may be a collection of special interest made by such a person, as the collection of early children's books, made by Angela Brazil, at Coventry. The works of a local author are the subject of special collections in many places. The Brontë collection at Keighley, the vast Shakespeare Memorial Library at Birmingham and the Francis Thompson collection at Preston, are examples. At Coventry the George Eliot collection includes first and other early editions and representative later editions of the works, translations into several foreign languages, programmes and scripts of stage, film and radio adaptations. Pictorial records of people and places associated with the novels, critical works in several languages and the scripts of lectures, are among other material for which a constant look-out is kept.

Chapter 3
Types of Material

LOCAL studies may be likened to a jigsaw puzzle, in which seemingly useless scraps make a picture when fitted together. The foregoing chapter will, it is hoped, have made it clear that the librarian of the local collection will need to cast his net widely to gather in all the information relevant to the study of the area in all its aspects, and the scraps will be as acceptable as the more substantial items. Frequent mention has been made of the 'material' on a particular topic; in the local collection this comprises a wider variety of types than in the general library. It is proposed to enumerate these types of material and to indicate some representative examples of each.

BOOKS AND PAMPHLETS

These, almost wholly the stock-in-trade of most of the other departments of the library, will form the bulk of the local collection, but the need to accumulate all the available information on a subject, however scanty, will result in a higher proportion of pamphlets than elsewhere. Among the books may be novels by local authors and criticism of their works, biographies, directories and historical works. Public or private records such as parish registers, hearth tax returns, the registers of some famous school, estate accounts and Quarter Sessions records, published by the local authority or historical society will probably be numerous. The library may be fortunate in acquiring copies of theses; these are frequently the only work on their subject and may come to be regarded as standard textbooks.

Some Government publications may deal exclusively with the area such as the *Memoirs of the Geological Survey* or Acts of Parliament promoted by the local authority for the granting of some special power. Together with an Act, the Bill, Minutes of Evidence and reports of any public meetings or referendum should be available. Other Government publications may be of wider application, but will be included in the collection for their references to the locality, such as the reports of the *Committee Appointed To Consider of the Several Petitions relating to Ribbon Weavers* of 1818 and the *Hand Loom Weavers Commission* of 1840, which are essential to anyone studying, for example, Coventry's ribbon industry. The books may also include publications of nongovernmental bodies such as *Conurbation*, the report of the West Midlands Group on Post-War Reconstruction and Planning.

As has already been said, pamphlets will constitute a considerable part of the local collection. In subject matter they will range over all fields of study and may often provide the only available information on their subject. Owing to the somewhat casual manner in which many are published, extreme vigilance is necessary to avoid overlooking them. Many of the pamphlets collected will probably be local authority publications including by-laws, handbooks for council house tenants, departmental annual reports and guides to such as the social services or youth service. Booklets issued in connection with some new project, such as an abattoir or to commemorate a landmark in a public service, for example, the centenary of the fire brigade or the nationalization of the gas undertaking, provide a great deal of valuable information in a condensed form. Central Government publications may be as various as Orders in Council constituting a new ecclesiastical parish, a patent for some local product or a report on a local industrial dispute by the Government 'trouble-shooter'. Programmes, providing a record of the social and cultural activities of the area, will include those of cultural societies, further education courses run by the local authority, Workers' Education Association or university extra-mural department, theatres, concerts, sporting events and conferences. Civic occasions such as a visit by Royalty, or the commemoration of an important historical event, like a battle or the granting of a charter, are usually opportunities for the production of pamphlets which should be preserved. Reports, balance sheets and probably publicity brochures will be forthcoming from banks, building societies and charitable institutions. Catalogues can be a mine of information. They may be of exhibitions, from mid-nineteenth-century industrial arts exhibitions to present-day trade fairs; of art treasures from the stately homes of the neighbourhood, of the works of local artists or of exhibitions held locally. Sale catalogues of land and houses, particularly on the break-up of great estates, provide information on land-use, on farms and old dwelling-houses. Manufacturers' catalogues of their products are valuable for the student of industrial history and sometimes, as in the case of Stevens' silk ribbon pictures, to the collector. Auctioneers' sale catalogues of letters, manuscripts or other items of interest associated with a local author, works of a local artist or some product of the locality, have an added interest if the prices realized are recorded. Social and political questions have always produced extensive pamphleteering and the library which has been able to gather over a considerable period those concerning the area will have valuable material for the historian. Such writings of the late nineteenth and early twentieth centuries are now very scarce and, in consequence, very costly. Much of the historical and descriptive literature of any locality is in the form of pamplets. Guides to churches, places with literary associations, castles, archaeological sites or stately homes and town guides are produced for sale to visitors and should all be in the library's collection. Civic societies, local history societies, some branches of the Historical Association and other groups frequently undertake the publication of short historical works dealing with their area and local amateur historians often publish privately the result of a lifetime's study. The writings of local poets are most likely to be published in pamphlet form, as are also short plays, written for local performance, such as the

Porch Plays, modern morality plays presented in the porch of Coventry Cathedral. A keen look-out for offprints can produce valuable additions for the collection. These may include such as a paper on some aspect of local geology contributed by an eminent geologist to a scientific journal, an account of a local experiment in municipal engineering delivered at a professional conference by an officer of the local authority, or a critical essay on the works of a local author by an American professor of English, published in the journal of his university's literary society.

SERIAL PUBLICATIONS

Much of the material coming into the local collection will be in the form of serial publications, most of them received regularly, but some casually, for the odd item of local interest they may include. Among the latter may be a trade journal with a feature article on a local industry or an architectural magazine reviewing extensively an important building. Many local institutions and societies regularly publish their proceedings, magazine or newsletter, varying from the well-produced publications of a university or a long-established regional archaeological society to a few stencilled sheets issued by a small cage-bird society. These reflect their members' wide range of interests in such local matters as natural history, canals, railways, the arts and recreational activities and often include important contributions by experts in their particular field of study. Most of the English counties have a magazine; these tend to emphasize social events, but frequently include articles on local people, places, or a way of life. Even the social reports may prove of historic value at some future date. Local authority publications, some fulfilling statutory requirements, have a value to the local collection long outlasting their immediate purpose. These include registers of electors, council and committee minutes, yearbooks, abstracts of the Treasurer's accounts and public relations newsletters. Files of timetables for all forms of transport operating within and in communication with the area should be preserved. Where these are published frequently, it will not be necessary to keep all, but issues should be kept when they show revisions of services or fares. Local educational establishments may account for many of the collection's serials. These may include university, polytechnic or college calendars, yearbooks or prospectuses and students' magazines together with magazines of schools of all grades within the area. In addition to providing a record of activities, some include biographical details of students which may assume added importance at a future date. For example, in gathering information on the poet Philip Larkin, a schoolboy essay by him was found in Coventry Grammar School magazine. In another field, reports of Rugby School Natural History Society record valuable observations on the geology, flora and fauna of the neighbourhood. Parish magazines, with their notices of baptisms, marriages and burials, obituary notices and notes on parish matters, including the fabric of the church are 'quarries' for future historians. For practical reasons of storage-space and usefulness, parts not concerned with local matters should be discarded. House journals produced by local firms, although sometimes largely snippets on staff matters, can serve a useful purpose in the local collection. They may contain articles on new processes, products or machinery or on matters of administration. Some, known to the author, carry long series of articles on various aspects of local history by amateur historians on the staff; others include valuable pictorial records by members of the firm's photographic society. Directories, general and special, are among the most widely-used publications in the local collection. Not all places are equally fortunate in the attention they have received from the publishers; lack of suitable businesses to provide advertising revenue has deprived some places of a reliable directory over a long period. Early nineteenth-century directories covered a wide area and were very limited in the information given, but the appropriate volumes should be collected from as early a date as possible. The Royal Historical Society's *Guide to the National and Provincial Directories of England and Wales . . .* 1950, details those published before 1856. In more recent times, the general and classified trade telephone directories partly fill the gap where town directories are lacking. Special directories will include diocesan directories (Church of England and Roman Catholic), directories for any trades carried on locally and any locally-compiled directories of a specialized nature, such as a directory of rural craftsmen.

NEWSPAPERS

Newspapers of all kinds have come to be regarded as one of the most valuable sources of history and this is especially true of local newspapers, particularly of the eighteenth and nineteenth centuries, when accurate reporting rather than sensation was the aim. Matters of public concern, such as sanitation and health, briefly noted in official reports, are fully ventilated. Negotiations for the making of canals and railways can be followed and details of their operation, with those of the turnpikes, gathered from the advertisement columns. Notices of sales of land are indicative of urban growth, workers' meetings of industrial unrest, and advertisements in an inland town of sailings to America of the interest in emigration. Obituary notices, detailed accounts of church restorations and, sometimes, articles on local history by a scholarly editor are among items to be found. Early newspapers have survived by virtue of the quality of the paper and the library not fortunate enough to possess complete files of its local newspaper can sometimes acquire batches, large or small, at sales. It can be helpful to have a record of the holdings of the newspapers of the area in other libraries, such as the British Museum Newspaper Library at Colindale or the Bodleian. Although the modern newspaper lacks many of the qualities of its predecessor, it is often the only source of current information and the library which maintains an indexed file of the local newspapers will be well equipped to handle enquiries relative to the present as well as to the past.

NEWSCUTTINGS

Scraps of information can be of the utmost value in local studies and newscuttings are the means of collecting and storing such scraps. Many libraries have profited from the magpie habits of local residents in this direction, by having had volumes of news-cuttings and scrapbooks donated. Some, lacking information as to date and source due to the method of mounting, are not as useful as might be wished, but are still worth having. One library, having lost its almost-complete files of local newspapers during the last war, was able to acquire a carefully-compiled series of local newscuttings covering about forty years up to 1905, thus replacing, in part, the wartime loss. Every local collection should make its own collection of cuttings. Where the current local newspapers are indexed, it is unnecessary to take cuttings in addition. However, there is an exception which can usefully be made. If there is an outstanding local event likely to attract extensive press coverage, both locally and nationally, cuttings might be collected, mounted together with any photographs and other relevant material and bound, making a useful volume on the subject. In this way Coventry produced four volumes on the new Cathedral, complete with index, covering the building from the cutting of the first sod until the consecration. A similar scrapbook was compiled to cover the festival held at the time of the consecration. Cuttings on local matters from other sources, such as national newspapers and periodicals, should be collected.

MAPS, PLANS AND CHARTS

Maps of all kinds are an essential source of information in many fields of local study, particularly to the historian and geographer.

From the Bodleian Library's crude so-called 'Gough' map of about 1330, of which reproductions are available, to the latest publications of the Ordnance Survey, all have a contribution to make. The early county maps, by Christopher Saxton, John Speed and others, beautiful examples of the engraver's art, are described in Thomas Chubb's *The Printed Maps in the Atlases of Great Britain and Ireland*. They throw light on places which have long since disappeared and the town plans printed as insets on the Speed maps are often the earliest known. John Ogilby's popular route maps, first published in his *Britannia* in 1675, provide much information on roadside features. From 1729, when Henry Beighton produced his 1-inch map of Warwickshire, great advances were made in the art of accurately surveyed map-making, culminating in the Ordnance Survey, which was undertaken to satisfy a military need.

The Ordnance Survey maps of England and Wales, beginning with the 1-inch first edition, published in 110 sheets between 1805 and 1873, have, with many revisions and new editions, recorded the changing landscape. The 25-inch series produced from the survey made between 1853 and 1893 and the 6-inch maps reduced from them have also undergone revisions, varying in frequency according to rapidity of change taking place. The 2½-inch map, introduced after World War II, meets the needs of those requiring a bridge between the 1-inch and 6-inch. Between 1843 and 1894 an urban survey was made and town plans produced on a scale of 5 feet and 10 feet to the mile. With the exception of London, for which only 5-foot plans were published, these became obsolete and were succeeded by 50-inch plans introduced in 1911. For some towns a special series of 10-foot plans were produced about 1850 at the town's expense, for use in sanitary engineering. A new series of 50-inch plans of major towns, started in 1943, is still in progress, with new sheets under continuous revision. Among other small-scale Ordnance Survey maps of use in local studies are the Period Maps, such as Roman Britain and Monastic Britain, and County Administrative Diagrams showing boundaries. 'A Guide

to Ordnance Survey Maps as Historical Sources' by J. B. Harley
and C. W. Phillips is to be found in the *Amateur Historian*, vol. 5,
nos. 5–8, 1962–3.

In addition to any Ordnance Survey town plans of the area,
all other town maps, from whatever source available, should
be collected and preserved as a record of change. There is often
need, both for present enquiries and as historic record, for
information not shown on any published map, such as boundaries of electoral wards and ecclesiastical parishes, or a clear
indication of the date at which certain areas were added during
a town's growth. With the co-operation of other bodies possessing this information, basic up-to-date maps may usefully have
the necessary boundaries drawn in by the library's staff.

Geological maps of the area, both drift and solid, produced
by the Geological Survey with the explanatory *Memoirs*, should
be included if possible. Unfortunately, some sheets are unobtainable, the plates having been destroyed during the last war and
not replaced. Soil Survey and coal-seam maps, where these have
been published, together with Land Utilisation Survey maps are
also essential.

The local authority will probably produce a variety of maps
and plans which should be added to the library's collection.
These may include programme maps for redevelopment, maps
prepared in connection with a local Act of Parliament, or some
new undertaking, defining smokeless zones or rights of way surveyed under the National Parks and Access to the Countryside
Act of 1949, and plans for projected buildings or the lay-out of
open spaces.

The opportunity should be taken of adding to the collection
plans of all kinds. In addition to published plans of local buildings collected from architectural and building journals, these
might also usefully include 'home-made' charts of, for example,
the figures in stained-glass windows, or those carved on some
public buildings, where published information is elusive.

PICTORIAL RECORDS

The value of photographs as a source of history and an essential form of record to be included in the local collection has been recognized by librarians since the early years of the present century. The eye of the camera frequently records features over-looked by the human observer and photographs not only supple-ment the written word but are often a more informative and easily-understood alternative. Many of the photographs taken in the early days of the art have survived in family albums or as negatives. The people and some of the places they depict have gone, but the Victorian scene has been recorded for posterity. The vogue of the commercially-produced picture postcard, which started at the end of the nineteenth century, has provided many libraries with valuable collections of street scenes, often showing buildings no longer existing of which there is no other record. The variety of subjects for photographic record is almost endless. They include everyday scenes of daily life such as marketing, children at play, city-centre rush-hour, the end of a shift at a coalmine, people at work in a factory or on the farm, the machines they operate and the goods they produce. Sporting and social events, ceremonial occasions, festivities and fairs; these, with the people taking part, their equipment and the clothes they are wearing, are material for the social historian. Photographs of trains, tramcars, buses, haulage vehicles and all other forms of transport, together with their stations and depots, are sources of transport history. Buildings should be recorded with an eye to architectural detail rather than pictorial effect. The biographical section of the local collection would be incomplete if it did not include portraits of all kinds of school groups, political gatherings, business and industrial groups, civic officials and prominent figures in all spheres of activity in the area.

It is understood that photographs, as applied to many of the subjects mentioned above, include also lantern slides and, in recent years, colour transparencies. In some respects these may be less suitable for reference use than prints but they serve a useful purpose and should be collected with the rest. Aerial photographs should also be included. Firms specializing in this work cover an area periodically and submit prints for sale. These can be particularly valuable when taken from a low altitude, when details of the buildings are clearly discernible. In areas of development and redevelopment, a series of photographs taken at intervals can be very informative. The value of aerial photographs in archaeological investigation has long been recognized and these should be included with other material on any sites in the area.

Prints and drawings should also be collected. Many of these will date from before the invention of photography and will be topographical, although there may be some portraits. Reproductions of line drawings illustrating local events, buildings or manufactured goods, such as watches or bicycles may be found in the *Illustrated London News* or trade journals of the nineteenth century. There may be an opportunity to acquire sketchbooks. These may have little artistic value but have a contribution to make towards a knowledge of the past.

BROADSIDES

Much valuable information on many aspects of local study is to be found in broadsides and these have been used as the principal source for some outstanding works. Every opportunity should be taken to collect not only old ones, but to select from the current outpouring those likely to be of interest in the future. In political history, lampoons, cartoons and chairing songs of the eighteenth and nineteenth centuries tell the story of rowdily-contested elections. Circulars, bills announcing meetings and candidates' addresses systematically collected provide material for the history of our time. A collection of playbills is theatre history. Places of performance, perhaps before the establishment of a

permanent theatre, public taste indicated by the plays performed, appearances of famous players, prices of admission, the
practice of giving performances for the benefit of a player or a
local charity, are among the information to be gathered. The
incidence of crime and treatment of criminals can be gleaned
from nineteenth-century bills announcing sentences passed and
the 'dying confessions' peddled on the occasion of the public
hangings. Handbills and posters giving public information on
such matters as air-raid precautions, feeding and health matters,
provide material for a study of the civilians' role during the last
war. Notices setting out the masters' 'iniquities' and calling
workers' meetings are a contribution to industrial history.
The occasional supermarket handbill could serve as a record
of current food prices, and posters, of cultural and social
activities.

MICROFILMS

The use of microphotography in libraries is especially adaptable
to the needs of the local collection and deserves to be used more
widely than it is. Many libraries have put their local newspapers
on to microfilm, reducing storage-space and wear and tear on
the papers which, in the case of early issues, have often become
fragile. This apart, full advantage is not generally taken of the
opportunity to add to the collection material not otherwise
available. The microfilms available from the Public Record
Office of the *Enumerators' Books* for the Censuses of 1841, 1851,
1861 and 1871 are invaluable. They provide not only a substitute for directories where, perhaps, none existed, but information for research in many fields, including industrial history and
genealogy. Arrangements may be made to procure in this way
much material, printed or manuscript, in private or public
ownership, relating to the locality. Unpublished works, including theses and diaries, may be borrowed for copying, sometimes
on condition that application for use is made to the owner.

Incomplete files of local newspapers may be made up with films of other holdings, public or private. Coventry replaced some nineteenth-century Government reports lost during the last war by microfilming borrowed copies. Where photocharging is in operation, extracts of local interest in books or periodicals could be photographed. When the reel is no longer needed by the lending library the appropriate strip could be cut out and a print made from it.

RECORDINGS

The recording of matters of local interest is not confined to printed or written and visual evidence but includes also sounds of great variety. The increasing use of tape-recorders and the widening of the field covered by gramophone recordings brings many aspects of local life within their sphere and the records they produce should have their place in the local collection. Gramophone records may be of performances of the works of a local composer, of a local choir or orchestra or of an outstanding musician, instrumentalist or vocalist. Music special to the area, such as country dances, folk-songs or carols, may be available. Records may be of speech, such as a lecture, a dramatic performance by a local actor or of the work of a local writer. Coventry has records of Philip Larkin reading his poems and of a lecture on George Eliot. They may be sounds of non-human origin such as bird-song from some wood in the area. Tape-recordings and their collection open up interesting possibilities. Local dialect, lectures, folk-song groups, public meetings or commentaries on sporting events can all be recorded and preserved on tape. Environmental sounds of our time, some of which are likely to disappear, might also be recorded, such as markets and fairs, tramcar bells and factory and workshop noises.

MUSIC SCORES

Scores for many of the musical items mentioned above will be available in published form or photocopies may be obtainable by co-operation with composers or performers from their manuscript copies. These should all be added to the collection.

Chapter 4

The Local Collection in relation to the Record Office, Museum, Art Gallery and Other Libraries

THE study of an area in all its aspects and at all levels requires the use of materials more widely-ranging than those detailed in the foregoing chapter. In some places all or some of these may be included in the library's collection; in others they form separate departments, either jointly or separately administered. All serve a common purpose and are complementary, whatever their disposition. Some libraries have collections of local records; their timely collecting saved from destruction much valuable historical source material, before the establishment of record offices in recent years. In many towns too small to justify a record office, the library is the only place where local records can be collected for study purposes. Similarly, where there is no museum or art gallery, the library is often the repository for any museum or art specimens in the possession of the local authority. In places having a library, museum, art gallery and record office, each will pursue its own course in collecting, preserving and making available for study the material coming within its purview. The scope of each should be clearly defined, to avoid overlapping and competitive collecting. There should be the closest co-operation; collectively they provide the community they serve with all the materials for local study, whatever the field of interest.

The definition of archives as records made in the course of business may be taken as the line roughly dividing the material collected by the record office from that of the library's local collection. Many record offices have been established since the last war, and there is a tendency to extend their collecting to material generally considered as coming within the scope of libraries. Where a record office and a flourishing local collection exist in the same place, it is essential for the librarian and archivist to have an understanding as to what each shall collect. It would appear a logical step for a library which has acquired records during its longer existence to transfer them to the more recent record office, and to continue to direct there any such material coming into its possession. The archivist, in turn, would pass to the library material coming within the scope of the local collection. The division of primary sources to the record office and secondary sources to the local collection is not always valid, for not all primary material is archival. Many manuscript letters, autobiographies and diaries are the province of the local collection rather than of the record office.

The archivist, an officer of the clerk to the council – the legal custodian of the authority's records – will have charge of all original documents, old and modern, concerning all aspects of official business, including those concerning the law courts and medieval guilds, together with any transcripts of such records. He will also endeavour to collect the archives of private undertakings in the economic, industrial and social fields. The library will confine its collecting to the publications of these bodies intended for public perusal. For example, the original minutes of the council and its committees will be in the custody of the archivist, but the local collection will include the proceedings of committees for submission to council as circulated for public information. A local charity might deposit its account books in the record office, but its published balance sheets and reports would be in the library's collection. Maps and plans drawn in connection with the local authority's business are archives, but all others, including plans published by the authority as information to the public, come within the scope of the local collection. Local Acts of Parliament, together with any published reports, evidence or petitions will be available in the library, but the confidential reports of officers and all other documents relating to the drafting and passage of the Bill are material for the record office. An exception to this division of interest should be made in the case of the library's archives. Reports, correspondence and other documents may be working equipment for a long time; when this ends the librarian would appear to be the appropriate person to select those to be preserved in the local collection for historic record.

Both departments can be mutually helpful in dealing with enquiries. Written requests, particularly, are often received by each on matters coming within the scope of the other; the enquirer's interests are best served by passing on the request, informing him that this has been done. Some enquiries will involve the use of material in both collections, and the good relations existing between librarians and archivists will effect an exchange of information to satisfy, fully, the enquirer's needs. The staffs of the record office and of the local collection should keep themselves informed regarding the contents of each, including important new acquisitions. Any available catalogues or calendars of the other will assist them in offering advice to their readers. By working in close co-operation, the record office and the local collection can often acquire valuable new material which has been brought to the notice of the other.

Where a library has no bookbinding department, or staff trained in repair work, it may be possible to arrange for the record office to undertake some work for the local collection. The specialist knowledge needed for the preservation of documents requires the services of trained workers, with accredited materials and equipment. Most record offices have provision for this work; most local collections have not but, with co-operation, expert advice might be forthcoming and a limited amount of special work carried out.

In many places with both a library and a museum, the office of librarian and curator is traditionally a joint one. The diversity of duties, coupled with restricted funds, often produce a tendency for one department to be developed at the expense of the other, according to the special interest of the officer. With the widening scope of museum activities, developments in their administration and facilities for staff training, more local museums have been established in recent years and qualified curators appointed. They are often administered jointly with the library, with a director as the officer responsible for overall control. The relics of the past, preserved and displayed in the museum, and the written material in the local collection about them and the people who made or used them complement each other in contributing to a knowledge of the history of the locality, and the closest co-operation is called for between the two departments. Movement of staff within the museum profession is, at least, as great as in the library profession, resulting in the appointment of newcomers to the district to the posts of curator or departmental keepers. An essential part of the equipment of workers in any department in the field of local studies is a background knowledge of the history of the place. Members of the museum staff should be afforded every facility for acquiring this knowledge from the material in the local collection; if possible by the long-term loan to the museum of duplicate copies of basic histories.

The dividing line is more clearly defined between the material in the local collection and in the museum than is the border line with the record office. As with local records, an old-established library may have acquired in its early years objects which are rightfully museum specimens; these, too, should be transferred. Some instances suggest themselves of possible items coming within the scope of either department and requiring an agreement on collecting practice. A library with a special collection of works by and about a local author may have acquired, in addition to printed material and manuscripts, personal possessions of the author or other association items. The student of literature will expect to find the written material in the library; the visual objects would appear to be museum items. Ideally, the collection should be kept together, but practical considerations of facilities for exhibiting it should be the deciding factor. Books printed in the locality are to be found in most local collections, but they might justifiably be collected by the museum. If the place has been an important centre of printing, the museum will probably build up a collection on the industry and books would be as essential a part as motor-cars are to the engineering industry.

The separation of related material between the local collection and the museum need be no bar to its collective use. Frequent opportunities will present themselves for the local collection to contribute material to be exhibited in the museum, supplementing the items available there. A landmark in the history of a local school might be such an occasion. An old-time uniform worn at the school, from the museum's collection, has an added interest if it is displayed together with photographs of the school buildings and groups of scholars and of teachers, the school magazine and any other items from the library's collection. The museum's medals, mugs or plates, perhaps made for presentation to local schoolchildren to commemorate a coronation, might be placed in context with contemporary photographs and programmes of local events celebrating the occasion. The loan collections provided by some museums for circulation among schools might usefully be supplemented by material from the local collection.

The museum staff will need to make constant use of the local collection in gathering background information to the objects collected, for compiling catalogue entries and display labels. Finds in a demolished building raise questions regarding its former use; regalia worn by an officer of a friendly society requires notes on the history and objects of the society; botanical specimens may need to be checked against earlier recordings in proceedings of the local natural history society or the local *Flora*. The exhibits in an industrial museum demand a knowledge of the industry as carried on locally and of the men who produced them; the uniforms of civic officials, the duties and holders of the offices. Postal enquiries received by the museum will often need the assistance of the staff of the local collection in producing the required information, and enquiries addressed to the library may need information about items in the museum to supplement that available in the local collection. Material for the preparation of catalogues and other museum publications, issued in connection with exhibitions, will probably be largely drawn from the local collection; any work done by the library staff will be recompensed with copies of the publications for addition to the collection. The addition of a brief bibliography of material used would be good publicity for the local collection. Offprints of any papers on items of special interest, contributed by the museum staff, should also be available for addition to the library.

The archaeological work of the museum will require the closest co-operation from the local collection. Maps and plans, drawings and photographs, geological data, reports and historical articles will provide the documentary evidence necessary to the archaeologist. Material not normally loaned might be transferred for use in the museum while work is in progress; if the library and museum are in close proximity it could readily be recalled if needed. In return, the local collection would expect to receive copies of any reports or papers contributed by the archaeologist, together with photographs, plans or drawings of discoveries made.

The respective roles of the library and museums are not always clear to members of the public, and each will be approached regarding matters concerning the other. These may be requests for information or offers of donations or to sell. The curator and the librarian of the local collection will each know the resources of the other collection and will refer the enquirer, knowing that his requirements will be met.

The division of pictorial material between the library and the art gallery will depend on the purpose each item serves, rather than its medium. The library's collection will consist, principally, of prints and photographs, but some of these come within the scope of the art collection. The deciding factor in collecting should be whether an illustration provides an historic record or is an example of an art form. The local collection may include etchings for their topographical interest, but would leave the collection of artists' proofs and various impressions to the art gallery. The library will provide the art gallery with much of its data about its local pictures. Undated scenes can often be dated from documentary evidence and by comparison with other illustrations. Biographical information on local artists and historic notes on the places or events forming the subjects of pictures will be available to the art gallery staff. The local collection will benefit from co-operation by the acquisition of the art gallery's publications, such as exhibition catalogues, monographs on local artists and photographs of pictures.

The librarian of the local collection will keep in close touch with other libraries in the area concerned with local studies. These may be in a university or college; loans may be arranged, and it is sometimes possible to lend a helping hand by passing on information about material available, as a gift or for purchase, which is surplus to the collection's requirements. The local newspaper often maintains a library; good relations with the librarian can be a mutual advantage. One newspaper regularly puts its files on microfilm, allowing the library to have copies for the cost of the additional film. The local collection can become a focal point for all local studies; the librarian who knows what material is available elsewhere and maintains close co-operation with those who have charge of it, can ensure that an enquirer has access to everything available locally on his subject.

Chapter 5
The Acquisition of Material

THE special need of the local collection to accumulate both old and current material relating to the area in the past and at the present time, with an eye to meeting the requirements of the future, calls for considerable variation in the methods of acquisition from those in practice in the general library. Some of the standard sources of information on new publications are a guide to material specifically on the locality, but much that needs to be collected is more elusive and provides something of the excitement of the chase in tracking it down.

Regular checks should be made of the *British National Bibliography* although, owing to the delay, publications may often have been received from other sources before they appear there. The fact, too, that many publications of use in local studies fail to reach the Copyright Office results in their omission. The Historical Association's *Annual Bulletin of Historical Literature*, arranged chronologically, is also worth examining. For Government publications HMSO's monthly list should be checked. Local historical societies are frequently also record-publishing societies with membership giving entitlement to copies of any publications. Records so published usually include a scholarly introduction providing a key to their interpretation and an important contribution to the subject. Such societies generally have an institutional class of membership; apart from the receipt of publications, there are many advantages to be gained by the library becoming a member. Local authors, whether writing on local matters or otherwise, are always anxious for publicity for their work and send copies to the local newspapers for review. Editors are usually generous in giving notice to such publications, and in the systematic reading of the local newspapers which is an essential part of the local collection librarian's duty, a special look-out should be kept for such items. Local publishers frequently circularize the libraries in their area with news of forthcoming publications and the local booksellers will generally call attention to any they may receive.

Much of the most important research work on an area is never published, but after submission as a thesis to a university or college remains in the library, its use strictly limited. It is sometimes possible to make the work more widely available by procuring a copy for the local collection of the area concerned. This can be negotiated in the early stages of the work, when the student is using the resources of the local collection in collecting material. Friendly assistance paves the way for a suggestion that a copy would be a valuable addition to the collection and the offer of a contribution towards the cost of typing may be an additional inducement to agreement. Two geography theses acquired by Coventry in this way are in constant use; the complete sets of maps accompanying them are invaluable. Where such an arrangement cannot be made, it is often possible to obtain a microfilm from the university, with the consent of the author and subject to any reservations he may make. Guidance to the subjects of theses may be found in the annual reports of the Institute of Historical Research, where theses in progress are listed, in the indexes published by ASLIB, and for urban areas in the *Urban History Newsletter*, a twice-yearly stencilled publication edited by Dr Harold Dyos of the Department of Local History of the University of Leicester.

Arrangements should be made for the regular receipt of publications of the local authority. These will include council minutes, electoral registers, treasurer's estimates and abstract of accounts, yearbooks, departmental reports, development plans, programmes and brochures of civic events, rules and regulations and by-laws. Pamphlets and leaflets issued for public relations will include college prospectuses. Irregularity of publication dates and failure to observe requests for regular mailing makes it necessary to keep a close watch for items failing to arrive. The publication of departmental reports is usually reported to Council and minuted; by a regular reading of the minutes, an awareness of local government activities and keeping in touch with public relations and other departments the librarian of the local collection should be able to ensure that nothing is missed. Similar arrangements will apply to collecting the reports of other bodies, such as banks, building societies, hospitals, gas and electricity boards, charitable institutions and Co-operative Societies. Programmes of theatres, professional and amateur, concerts, sports and other recreational events, shows and exhibitions are other items which may be sent regularly, but reminders may be necessary periodically. Press reports of events, including annual meetings of societies and organizations, will keep the librarian informed and a wide range of outside interests among members of the staff may bring in much useful material. Auctioneers' and estate agents' catalogues are usually forthcoming on application; the enclosure of a stamp for return postage is appreciated. In addition to notices in the local newspapers the property advertisements in *Country Life* are worth scanning for the announcements of sales of country houses.

Serial publications will be acquired in various ways. Some will come by virtue of membership of a local historical or archaeological society which regularly publishes its transactions. Others may be subscribed for to a university or learned society, or be commercially published and purchased from a local dealer. Many will be gifts, either solicited or offered by an editor who may have friendly relations with the local collection. Requests may be made in writing, but a telephone call is often found to be more effective. Among those to be approached are secretaries of societies, heads of schools, incumbents of parishes and publicity managers of industrial concerns. The latter are sometimes very generous in supplying not only their journal as issued, but a bound volume, with index, annually. It may be necessary to make payment, for example for a parish magazine, but most are likely to be presented. Constant check needs to be kept for receipt, for changes of secretary or cessation of publication are often responsible for a failure in delivery.

Much of the information of use in local studies is to be found in newspapers and periodicals and perseverance in searching can be rewarding. However, there are several aids to lighten the task. The *British Humanities Index* arranges articles under local headings. The *Regional Lists*, reprinted from the *Index*, were handy guides but these were discontinued in 1966. The *British Technology Index* provides references to articles on any local industries and other technological matters. Both books and periodical articles on an outstanding local author may be traced in the *Annual Bibliography of English Language and Literature* and in the *Year's Work in English Studies*. The Council for British Archaeology's *Archaeological Bibliography for Great Britain and Ireland* lists, under counties, archaeology and a wide range of allied subjects. A routine check of any periodicals received in the reference library which are not included in these works will often produce material. *Country Life* is a valuable source for articles on the great houses, well illustrated and often extending over several issues, and on other matters of local interest, including the replies to collectors' questions. Although this is indexed, it is still advisable to check, for items which may not appear to have local significance to an indexer frequently have for someone with local knowledge. National newspapers such as *The Times*, *Daily Telegraph* and the *Guardian* and the *Sunday Times* and *Observer* often have feature articles on provincial towns or some local institution. The correspondence columns and obituary notices should not be overlooked, neither should *The Times* reviews of pamphlets. Watchful members of the staff can be of great assistance in gathering in fugitive information.

The *Publications Report*, regularly issued by the Ordnance Survey, provides up-to-date posting of new sheets in all scales, including geological maps. Many maps and plans will be produced by the local authority in connection with its variety of responsibilities. The local collection librarian should keep well informed, by reading council minutes and establishing good relations throughout the local government service, of all that is happening and ensure that copies of any maps and plans available for public consultation are added to the collection. Commercially produced town plans will be on sale at bookstalls and bookshops; regular browsing among these can be profitable.

The collection of photographs, which will form the bulk of the pictorial material, can be a combination of planning and opportunism. In many places photographic societies have, from time to time, undertaken to make a photographic survey of the area, sometimes to a schedule drawn up by the local librarian, and deposit prints in the library; Coventry acquired in this way a record of the places associated with George Eliot's novels. Unfortunately, interest is not usually sustained and in many cases this source of supply has failed. Although formal arrangements may have broken down, it is sometimes possible to arrange through a photographic society for one of its members to record a particular subject, such as a building about to be demolished. Payment for film is usually all that is required. Some libraries have organized schemes for systematically recording the topography, architecture and events of their area. Where funds are available this is ideal, but not all can achieve it. It could be claimed that the function of the library is to collect records and not to create them. Equally, there exists a public duty to record the changing landscape. The planning and public works departments are, perhaps, the best qualified for programming photographic recording, while the library would seem to be the most suitable place to house the collection. The most satisfactory way of dealing with this would be a co-operative scheme, separately financed.

The absence of such a scheme is no bar to the accumulation of a useful collection, but rather more contriving is called for. The local press can be very helpful. In exchange for information provided by the staff of the local collection in connection with some matter of historic interest which is in the news, prints will often be presented of photographs taken to accompany a report. In addition, reports of important local events are usually well covered by photographs and obituary notices accompanied by portraits; prints of these may be purchased. Reader-interest can sometimes be the means of procuring copies of old photographs. One local newspaper published several interesting old photographs and invited readers to submit for possible publication any they had. Great numbers were sent in and many published. Through the co-operation of the newspaper the owners of both published and unpublished photographs were approached; in some cases they gave the prints to the library, others lent them for copying.

Exhibitions of photographic societies sometimes include a section of prints or transparencies of local interest. By regularly visiting such exhibitions, useful prints can often be acquired from the exhibitor, sometimes by gift. Where the local collection covers a rural area, it can be worthwhile visiting the village history exhibitions which are increasingly being held. These often produce treasure for the historian in the form of photographs and other material long hidden away. For the librarian who shows a friendly interest they may bring gifts to the collection or the opportunity of copying photographs and other rare material. Periodic displays of a selection from the library's collection will arouse the interest of collectors or photographers who are often willing to contribute prints or negatives to the collection or lend them to be copied. Photographs of buildings and architectural features throughout the country are preserved in vast numbers in the collections of the National Buildings Record, the Royal Commission of Historical Monuments and the Royal Institute of British Architects, from which copies are available for purchase.

Information about gramophone recordings may be found in the *Gramophone, Record Review* and the *New Records*. As in many other items, the local press is a valuable source, for most discs of local interest will be sent for review. Again, personal contact can be of great assistance, especially if the library has a gramophone record lending library. Many of the borrowers will have knowledge of local activity in making recordings and readily pass on information. The local record dealer will also be helpful in calling attention to any recordings of local interest. The acquisition of tape-recordings is another matter in which the co-operation of local residents can be a great asset. Tape-recording societies are rapidly increasing in numbers and are to be found in most areas. They are usually very willing to make recordings if the cost of tapes is met. The consent of any speaker or performer must be obtained and the rules of copyright observed. As in other departments of the library, readers' requests can often be a means of acquiring stock. Enquirers frequently have knowledge of some out-of-the-way publication, perhaps by acquaintance with the author or publisher or a special interest in the subject. The library can be best served in collecting new material for its local collection by a staff with a lively interest in all the activities of the area and an enquiring and acquisitive nature.

The collection of out-of-print material cannot be planned, as in the case of much of the current material added to the local collection, but must be largely a matter of keeping a sharp lookout in order to avoid missing anything. Secondhand bookshops are an obvious source of supply and regular visits should be paid to any in the vicinity. No opportunity for browsing in shops in other areas should be lost, for books of local interest are often to be found far from the place they concern and, frequently, at a lower price. In some of the lists sent out by secondhand booksellers books are arranged under regional headings, but items concerning the locality in some aspect may be found elsewhere in the list. A telephone call immediately on receipt of a catalogue often avoids the disappointment of losing a wanted item by the delay of posting an order. Photograph albums, scrapbooks and other oddments from the home of an old person who has died often find their way into a local 'junkshop'; something of use to the local collection may be found to make an occasional call worthwhile.

In most areas a great deal of material on the locality, some of it very rare, is in the possession of local residents. The librarian will take every opportunity of making their acquaintance and of knowing what the collections include. This sometimes leads to gifts and bequests or offers to sell; in any case the knowledge is useful in the eventuality of a sale. The libraries of country houses which have been in the ownership of a family for centuries often have long files of local newspapers; means have been found of making purchases from such accumulations to fill gaps in the local library's collection. A close watch should be kept on auction sales, both locally and in London. Arrangements can be made for firms such as Sotheby's to supply catalogues of sales including material in a particular field of interest. An inspection should be made prior to the sale and agreement reached with any other party known to be interested.

A file of wanted items might usefully be kept. This could include, in addition to material not in the collection, extra copies of books already on stock required for lending or possible replacement. A local bookseller is often able to supply such wants by circularizing the trade. A request in the correspondence column or a 'wants' advertisement in the local newspaper have been known to produce several copies of a still popular town history long out of print, some as gifts, others for sale.

Developments in methods of photo-reproduction are making it increasingly possible to acquire for the local collection material not otherwise obtainable. Articles in periodicals, early Acts relating to canals and railways, official reports and maps are among the items in public or private ownership from which it may be possible to have copies made.

Many local collections have had the benefit of gifts, large or small, indeed some have started from the donation of a private collection. The library which has built up a reputation for its local collection by service and publicity, will be held in high public esteem and the knowledge that material has been accumulated over the years and from many sources to provide the answer to almost any question on local matters, offers an inducement to local residents to make their contribution. The break up of an old family home often produces hoards of miscellaneous material stored away and long forgotten; repair work in a house may reveal papers secreted under floor boards; men working on the demolition of old property may find old photographs, books and papers. If the library has succeeded in making the public aware of the use to which such items may be put, they will automatically be brought in. Not all may be of use; material should be accepted on this understanding and agreement made to return or destroy it if not required. Donations should be acknowledged immediately by letter. Press reports on gifts of special interest, which may follow a minuted report to the library committee, are good publicity and may serve to attract others. A tradition of service may take a long time to establish; the newer libraries will be at a disadvantage in this, but by keeping in close touch with all sections of the community and procuring from any available source and assembling material to meet their needs, the building of a local collection can be very rewarding.

Chapter 6
Preparation for Use

FOREGOING chapters will have made it plain that the accumulation of material for a local collection is not undertaken merely to preserve it, but to provide a source from which a wide variety of people may draw for an equal variety of purposes. The extent to which all the books and non-book material gathered will be used, depends very much on the methods adopted to ensure that every item is readily available to provide for all enquirers the information it contains, for whatever purpose it is required or however the enquiry may be framed. Wealthy though a collection may be in material, its value to readers is only to be measured by the steps taken to exploit it. Unlike all other departments of the modern public library, material added to the local collection will only in very exceptional cases be discarded. The information it provides may well be superseded, but it will be retained as a contemporary record. The permanence and special nature of the collection requires procedures for recording its acquisition and making known its resources distinct from those applying to other departments, where stock is constantly changing and simplification of record-making a practical necessity. Many modern library practices, developed to speed up the process of making large numbers of new books available to readers in the shortest possible time, and for cataloguing them briefly, but adequately for their short life in the library, do not meet the specialized requirements of the local collection. Standardized practice cannot be applied to much of the material; the use to be made of each item determines its treatment. What that use is likely to be is best known to those working in the field of local studies and processing should be their responsibility.

The ordering and receipt of purchased books, pamphlets, maps and other material, new or secondhand, is most rationally carried out in the library's centralized book-order department, where some simplified system is probably in use for linking each briefly identified item with the order and invoice, serving all general requirements including those of the authority's payments and audit sections. After the addition of such identification mark as the system allots, all local collection items should be passed to that department for further processing. The brief recording of accessions at the ordering stage is inadequate for the local collection; everything added will, so far as is predictable, be there for all time and a full and permanent record of its accession should be kept.

Much of the material added to the collection will be acquired as donations and will need to be recorded, together with purchases. The miscellaneous nature of the material makes it practicable to maintain two registers, one for books and pamphlets and a separate one for all non-book material. The progressive number of each entry becomes the accession number for that item. Blocks of numbers distinguishing the two sequences may be assigned or some symbol, such as (M) for Miscellaneous, inserted between the departmental symbol and the number if two concurrent sequences are used.

For books and pamphlets information recorded should include, in addition to the accession number, the date of addition, author, title, volume number, publisher and place of publication if local, printer if local, date of publication, size, whether a book or pamphlet, the classification mark, a note on the binding if distinctive, the donor or vendor and price. Provision should be made for any necessary additional remarks, such as provenance or terms of a donation. In the rare cases of withdrawals from stock, numbers may be used again for dividing the accession number column for progressive and re-entered numbers. 'D' in the column before the number indicates that the item has been discarded and a note is added of the progressive number after which a new addition, with that number, is entered.

The register of miscellaneous material should record the accession number, date of acquisition, author (broadly connoted), publisher, place and date of publication, donor or vendor and price. In addition, columns should be provided for indicating the category of each item, whether a broadside, map, plan or chart, photograph, print, original drawing, lantern slide, recording or microfilm.

Not all additions will be accessioned as received. Serial publications will be bound when there are sufficient numbers to complete a volume, which can then be accessioned. Meanwhile, a record should be kept of what has been received, to serve also as a check against non-receipt; 5 in. × 3 in. ruled cards, filed alphabetically by title, behind guides indicating frequency of publication, serve this purpose. Details should include the title, frequency and, if regular, date of publication, source of supply and its location in the collection. The remainder of the card may be ruled into columns for recording the receipt of each issue. If a card is to continue in use after a volume is completed, the parts bound should be indicated.

Although, theoretically, nothing will ever be withdrawn from the local collection, it will occasionally be necessary to do so. Despite vigilance books are sometimes stolen; they often reappear but, if after a long period they are still missing, they must be written off. Similarly, books lent in good faith may disappear together with their borrowers. A register of withdrawals should be kept, recording the date of withdrawal, accession and classification numbers, author and title and the reason for withdrawal.

Just as the material comprising the collection is expected to last for all time, so must its records. The accessions and withdrawals registers should be kept in stoutly-bound ledgers, specially made with rulings for their purpose.

CLASSIFICATION

Opinion on what constitutes a satisfactory scheme for arranging the varied material in a local collection, for use by staff and readers, differs widely. Some hold that Dewey, and the other classification schemes in general use in libraries, are unsuited to the special requirements for accommodating all the material on the many aspects of study of a given locality; in particular, that the *Decimal Classification* does not provide for subdivision by subject under place headings. Many believe that differing arrangements within the library system are confusing to readers and staff, and use the same classification throughout, the majority of them Dewey. A number have devised their own schemes, including that for the Guildhall Library's collection of London Literature, upon which several others have been based. The late J. L. Hobbs detailed these in his *Local History and the Library*, with the addition of notes on their availability. Others use one of the standard schemes, with adaptations suited to the scope and content of their particular collection.

One such adaptation was made at Coventry by the late Dr E. A. Savage. Whether it was of this that he wrote he 'was a sinner come to repentance' is not known but, basically, it is still satisfactorily in use. The schedules were lost with all other records during the last war and it was necessary to reconstruct them around the classification numbers on surviving material. It was founded on the dictum that in a local collection 'place is paramount'. The collection covers the county of Warwick, and every administrative area within each of the ancient hundreds was assigned a two-letter notation by means of permutations on all the letters of the alphabet. This has the advantage of bringing adjacent places in close proximity on the shelves, although it breaks down for neighbouring places in different hundreds. As an example, AB denotes the county as a whole; HL Elmdon, HS Meriden, HU Solihull; JN Coventry, JO Stoke, JZ Foleshill. Stoke and Foleshill are now within the Coventry City boundary, but they have long histories as separate communities and it serves a useful purpose to group the relevant material under each. A deviation from the geographical arrangement makes special places for Shakespeare at TL, adjacent to Stratford-upon-Avon TM, and George Eliot at GM, next to Nuneaton at GN. Within the place divisions, subdivision is by subject according to Dewey, giving a mixed but comprehensible notation.

What is deemed to be the subject for the purpose of classifying the local collection is not always, strictly, the matter of the work. For books by local authors, on subjects other than those of local interest, the subject is authorship. Coventry's use of 013 for this is, perhaps, a little unorthodox but convenient; the Cutter-Sanborn tables are used for arranging authors alphabetically. Similarly, books printed before 1850, whose only local connection is the printer, are classified as rare books at 094, subdivided alphabetically according to the printer. Books from the library of a local celebrity or institution would have their place in a local collection for their association, rather than their subject, and would be classed as Ex Libris, 097 in Dewey. Works of pure literature are only likely to be placed in the form classes if they concern the locality in a general way; where the theme is some local event or personality, they are more usefully classified with the appropriate subject, such as Clemence Dane's *Scandal at Coventry*, a radio play, with other versions of the Godiva legend. Biographies may either be grouped together in the Biography class, subdivided by the Cutter-Sanborn tables, or classified according to the associated subject. They may make an important contribution to the literature of their subject; a satisfactory solution would be to classify them as Biography, making added entries in the catalogue under appropriate subjects.

It will probably be found, dependent on the local emphasis of a particular subject, that expansion or adaptation of the schedules is necessary in some classes. This may be contrived from a personal knowledge of the subject or by utilizing such as UDC expansions. Selected headings from J. D. Stewart's *Tabulation of Librarianship* conveniently arrange material on various local libraries, public and private, under the appropriate class numbers. Dewey's *Table for School and College Publications*, appended to the Education schedules, provides useful subdivision of an extensive collection in that class. Where the primary division is by place, Dewey's 900 will accommodate general histories; 909, Universal History, with its chronological subdivisions, is a suitable placing for historical works on a particular period. Other places may be found, perhaps distasteful to the purist, where adaptations may be made to meet local requirements.

Some types of non-book material may be accommodated in the classification scheme in general use; others will require special treatment. Broadsides and loose-leaf newscuttings adapt themselves to subject classification as separate items, and may be arranged in class order according to the method of storage in use. Maps are most usefully arranged by place, with subdivisions for such subjects as geology, land use and soil surveys. Those in series, as the Ordnance Survey, have a built-in classification by scale, edition and sheet number. Town plans and early county maps may conveniently be arranged in chronological order. If the collection, generally, is classified by place, subdivided by subject, this may be used for the illustrations collection, although it will probably be necessary to make some expansions. A large collection of photographs of town streets, for example, for convenient use need to be subdivided by name, viewpoint and date, and buildings by purpose, name, external and internal features, viewpoint and date. Some system for denoting such subdivisions will need to be devised for addition to the class mark.

Special collections require an arrangement inherent in the subject of the collection. For an author collection a scheme is needed to cover his works, life, criticism of his works and other material. The works might be subdivided into the forms in which he wrote, such as novels, essays, poetry, literary criticism or translation, and would include epitomes, adaptations, printed and perhaps vocal, and translations. The life would include biographies, diaries, autobiography, letters and, perhaps, biographies of family and friends who influenced the author's writing. Critical works might include reviews, addresses and exercises in literary detection and geography. Miscellaneous material might include personal possessions, such as books that had influenced him, illustrations of people and places associated with his life and works, catalogues of sales of his works. Every collection will be peculiar to itself and a scheme of arrangement must be specially designed to fit it.

CATALOGUING

Although the local collection depends much on the knowledge of the staff to assemble all the material relevant to any enquiry, a comprehensive catalogue is essential to provide not only a means of self-help for readers but a key for the staff, in particular those who may lack familiarity with the stock. Its effectiveness will be proportionate to the extent to which each item is recorded to ensure it is brought to notice in connection with all matters to which it may relate. The librarian's knowledge of his readers' requirements and of the uses to which information may be put, makes him the best-fitted to compile a catalogue with the necessary wealth of detail. The provision of assistance to relieve him from some of the less skilled duties of the department, to enable him to do this, will be more than repaid by the ultimate saving of labour, coupled with increased efficiency.

It is not proposed to discuss here the details of practical cataloguing, or the form and physical production of the catalogue, that has been amply covered elsewhere by others, but rather to indicate the special requirements of the fully-operative local collection catalogue. The 1967 edition of the *Anglo-American Cataloguing Rules* goes far in rationalizing modern cataloguing practice and bringing into conformity some of the variant practices frequently adopted in local collection catalogues, often the only catalogue of the library to provide full entries otherwise in accordance with the rules of cataloguing. They are particularly serviceable for their treatment of the non-book material which comprises so much of the local collection.

Analytical entries will account for a considerable proportion of the catalogue. Many composite works include information that might well be overlooked on some aspects of local history. Volume 1 of the *Victoria History of the County of Warwick* includes a section on flora and fauna and volume 2 on sport; these and many other sections in this work justify their inclusion in the catalogue under both author and subject. Meteorological observations are included in the annual reports of the Medical Officer of Health for Coventry, a source almost certainly missed but for an analytical subject entry in the catalogue, and the famous Coventry Carol calls for an analytical entry from the medieval Pageant of the Sheremen and Taylors of Coventry. A collected work on the biographies of local celebrities should have analytical entries made for each. The publications of local record publishing societies often include lengthy authoritative introductions concerning the organization which produced the record; these also should be separately catalogued. Material for such entries is not confined to books. The earliest map of Coventry is Speed's, published as an inset to his map of Warwickshire, of 1610. The proceedings of local societies, journals of institutions and everything coming into the collection should be examined closely and catalogued to ensure that all the information it is capable of providing is recorded.

Added entries provide a further means of making the catalogue more informative. Most libraries, in their tendency to simplify cataloguing, omit some of the added entries prescribed by the rules. The cataloguer of the local collection will probably consider it expedient to include more. As an example, the report of a group study in environmental planning might name six local architects who contributed; from a local interest point of view, all should be named in the catalogue entry and an added entry appear under the name of each. Local printers, publishers and booksellers who are sometimes named on the title-page of early books, together with bookbinders named on an added label, may justify added entries, together with outstanding editors of newspapers and serials. Series entries might usefully be made for the publications of learned societies or other bodies, produced at intervals under a collective title. Perhaps of greater value are the added subject entries which should be plentifully provided. A thesis on the geography of Coventry providing information on ribbon weaving, watchmaking and the cycle and motor industry would be entered under each. The subject of a biography may have influenced more than one sphere of local life; the catalogue should place this on record.

The local collection catalogue will provide a great deal of additional information in the form of annotations, which are likely to be more extensive than in that of the general library. Many entries will need a full contents note to define the scope of the work and to serve as a key to analytical entries. Ambiguous titles, particularly of early writings such as religious or political tracts and of imaginative writing, will require explanation; a note on the inclusion of some unusual feature on a map would assist the searcher. Any information which contributes to a fuller understanding of the contents of a work should be added. Notes on the author are likely to be numerous; for a local author these are not necessarily confined to his qualifications for writing, but may be added to provide useful biographical information. For additional interest, his dates and any epithet should be included in the author heading. Entries for reports and surveys gain by the addition of a note on the investigators and the purpose and scope of the enquiry, or a textbook by the teacher-author's intention in writing it. Special copies of books might have notes added on the binding, illustrations or other features of bibliographical interest, or on previous ownership by a local celebrity or institution. Information on bibliographers, addenda and appendices indicate added usefulness to the reader and the insertion of any additional matter – manuscript, printed or illustrative – and any imperfections should also be noted.

Early works should be given full bibliographical descriptions with transcription of the title-page and statement of imprint and collation as prescribed in Esdaile's *Students' Manual of Bibliography*. The reference number of any entry of the work in a standard bibliography might be given in a note.

INDEXING

The main catalogue of the collection will probably include a considerable amount of material in addition to books and pamphlets, such as microfilms and recordings, most of which are, in effect, books or pamphlets with a different make-up, but there remains much to be recorded if a comprehensive guide to the resources of the collection is to be provided. This may be effected by the compilation of indexes which are better suited to some types of material, particularly if the catalogue is classified.

Most libraries maintain indexes to illustrations apart from the main catalogue; in some places prints, original drawings, photographs and slides are treated separately, but one index for all pictorial material would seem to be more practicable. For most purposes, the medium of an illustration, which will be stated, is of secondary importance and, if the location of each appears in the entry, a wanted item can be readily found with a minimum of searching. Illustrations should be fully catalogued, as prescribed by the rules but, in practice, most local collection enquiries are for subjects rather than artists, engravers or photographers. In collections which include the works of outstanding illustrators, entries under their names are essential, but in other cases arrangement under alphabetical subject headings proves very satisfactory. Some items illustrate more than one subject and the fullest use can be made of them by adding entries under each heading. For example, close-up photographs of carved wooden roof bosses in the medieval Guild Hall at Coventry show angels playing musical instruments. These are of interest in the study of the architecture of the hall, of medieval wood-carving and musical instruments and are entered in the index under those headings. Much pictorial material is likely to be scattered throughout the collection in books, magazines and newspapers; if time can be found to include this in the index its usefulness will make the effort worthwhile.

Maps may be conveniently catalogued separately, giving the prescribed information arranged to enable them to be traced by author-cartographer, engraver or publisher, and place or subject. In addition, indexes are essential for use with Ordnance Survey 6-inch and larger-scale maps, particularly if the collection includes all the editions. An index to places on the 6-inch and streets and, perhaps, some buildings on the 25-inch and larger, giving sheet numbers of the various editions, is not only a great time-saver for the searcher but reduces the wear and tear of handling the maps. A useful addition in the case of town maps would be references to changes of street names, which can often be very confusing. An index found very useful at Coventry is a street index to ecclesiastical parishes; this is combined with an index to the register of electors published separately by wards, with addenda lists made as new streets are built. Stencilled copies were produced for use at all the city libraries, but a surprising number of requests to purchase have been received from outside.

An index to the local newspapers is one of the most valuable pieces of equipment the local collection can have. Newspapers provide the latest, though perhaps not always accurate, and sometimes the only information on a subject and a key to their use provides a means of satisfying many enquirers. Some places maintain separate biographical indexes, but one sequence for all matters would appear preferable. Indexing is best done regularly as the paper is issued, for enquiries are often received within days of the event. Local circumstances will influence the matters indexed and the choice and form of headings; 5 in. × 3 in. cards, written in indian ink for permanence, are satisfactory for briefly recording the news item and its location.

Broadsides may be indexed under subject, and author or title. Some in series, such as playbills or Air Raid Precautions circulars, may be treated collectively.

Other regular indexing will include any volumes of news-cuttings or scrapbooks compiled by the staff on such matters as the Libraries Department, the Art Gallery and Museum where combined, or some outstanding event. Useful information can often be lost within the pages of, perhaps, a county magazine or house journal of a local firm which does not produce an index. If these are regularly noted as the issue is received, a typewritten index can be included when the parts are sent for binding.

The collection will, doubtless, include much more that requires indexing to reveal its contents. Many libraries will have acquired invaluable cuttings books whose compilers, if they considered indexing at all, entered such an item as one headed *A Shocking Accident* under A. Coventry has indexed several large gift collections, including one of some fifty volumes, and also a comprehensive standard history of the city published a century ago. Stencilled copies of the last are included in all copies of the book, which is in most of the city's libraries; this also has been sold to members of the public. The microfilm copies of the Census *Enumerators' Books* can be more easily used if a street index to the bundle numbers is provided.

A useful index can be compiled of material on the area, but not in the local collection. This may be sections in books in other departments of the library or books and other material in public or private ownership. For the latter it would be helpful to enquirers if information could be available concerning any facilities for access to it. Such an index might be kept separately or incorporated in a general index, with cards of a distinguishing colour.

The librarian of the local collection will be aware of the need for other indexes to inform his readers and the staff of the whereabouts of all the minutiae the collection includes. Only pressure of work is likely to prevent him from ensuring that these are provided.

LABELLING

The methods in general use in other departments of the library for marking the ownership of books, and to indicate their location on the shelves and other storage places, will need to be modified in the case of some local collection material. The treatment of rare and valuable books is mentioned in Chapter 7. Similarly, original drawings, rare prints and manuscripts should not be defaced by rubber or embossing stamps or numbering in ink; any necessary numbering should be either pencilled, on a label lightly tipped to the item or on a backing sheet or folder.

The collection will probably have its own departmental bookplate, in most cases pasted inside the front board. Where this has been used for annotations or inscriptions, for the bookplate of a previous owner or for an endpaper with any printed matter contributory to the work, the bookplate should be tipped in.

Donation should be recorded by the addition of a label in the work concerned. This may be a small label, with the name of the donor and the date, either pasted or tipped inside the back board, according to its value. A special collection, whether acquired by purchase or as a bequest, will probably have its own label for insertion in all items. In addition to acknowledging generosity, such labels serve as a reminder that contributions to the collection are acceptable.

Chapter 7
Accommodation and Treatment

WHATEVER the extent of the local collection or the refinement of accommodation provided for it, the basic requirements will be the same; adequate space for the variety of fittings needed to accommodate the many types of material constituting the collection, working-space both for the short-stay reader and the student making a prolonged study, safe storage for valuable material and working for staff, with provision for oversight. The amount of space provided, its allotment for the various requirements and the lay-out within those areas differs widely, not always in accordance with the size of the library. In some libraries, particularly new ones, the department occupies a considerable area and includes study rooms, a muniment room, strong room, exhibition room and study carrels, planned to accommodate an expanding service to meet the requirements of the increasing numbers who are being attracted to local studies. In many others, one room has been made available and adapted to house the collection and turn its use to good account.

As in all library planning, the use to be made of the department will, so far as is possible, determine its location within the building. The needs of the student, requiring a quiet place to work, will be the first essential; in a new library this can be provided for at the planning stage, but an older library will need to adapt to the best advantage. The department should be situated as far away as possible from street noises and from the traffic of the public using other busy departments, such as the adult and children's lending libraries. The frequent use made of the reference library and the need for material to be brought from stock and the strong room makes it desirable for these to be as near as possible. The atmospheric conditions required for the safe storage of valuable books and other material necessitates the closest attention to heating and ventilation, both in planning for the department in a new library and adaptation in an older building. A necessary provision, seldom found in older libraries, is toilet facilities for the public.

Within the limitation of the space available, as many tables and chairs as possible should be provided, allowing for a passage between them and access to the shelves while avoiding disturbing the occupants. In the one-room library, study tables are better placed as far as possible from the entrance and the counter, where activity can be distracting. If these can be situated at one end of the room, more space is available for concentrated study. A low screen across the room near the entrance, possibly incorporating the catalogue, panels for the display of prints or photographs, or shelving for frequently-used reference books, would provide a measure of seclusion for the serious student, while permitting oversight from the staff enclosure. The part of the room nearer the door, also under staff supervision, could accommodate the short-stay reader. Where floor space is restricted, square tables are generally more useful than oblong ones. If these are about 3 ft. × 3 ft., they will accommodate four readers using one or two books and are especially useful for schoolchildren or students working together. They provide sufficient space for at least two people with a fair complement of books and will accommodate the majority of maps. If they are of a uniform size and lightweight, two can be joined together if the occasion requires it. Light-coloured furniture presents a less forbidding appearance than dark; melamine or formica tops can look attractive and are practical and easily cleaned, but the liking for white should be resisted, as being trying to the eyes for a long period of study. Chairs should be chosen for comfortable use rather than ingenuity of design, and should give support for the back. The splayed legs of many modern chairs tend to occupy a great deal of floor space. Working-space for staff, apart from the counter, can be contrived by arranging double-sided shelving to form partitions. Some material to be produced on request, but not requiring strong-room protection, can be accommodated on the staff side and the staff are able to work without distracting readers. A busy local collection necessitates frequent use of the telephone. This should be positioned in such a way as to avoid its use within public hearing, if possible, but without the necessity of, perhaps, the one member of the staff on duty having to leave readers without supervision. The room must be well lit, with good natural lighting during daylight hours, if possible, although this may not always be consistent with the other requirements to be met for siting. Power points should be provided in suitable positions in the public and staff areas for the use of microfilm readers, reading lamps, cleaning and other working equipment.

Shelving in the public area should be confined to the walls; island bookcases and alcove arrangements encroach on space for study, create disturbing traffic and prevent oversight. Wooden cases are preferable to steel, which present an appearance of austerity inappropriate to the 'domestic' nature of the department. Some space should be available for pictures and other appropriate wall decoration and, possibly in the counter area or outside, for leaflets and posters referring to lectures, classes and other activities of local historical interest. Many local study departments will have little room to spare for exhibition cases and display screens. For small exhibitions, arranged by request for demonstration to groups, portable cases and screens might be brought in for the occasion. Other exhibitions are probably more effective if held elsewhere than in the department. The public side of the counter might usefully be fitted with cupboards for the convenient storage of stocks of publications available for sale.

STORAGE

The many types of material comprising the local collection require a variety of treatments for their safe storage and accessibility and to make the fullest use of available space. A survey of the books in the collection will indicate the size sequences necessary for the most economical use of shelf space. It may be advantageous to deviate from the standard measurements, 11 in. octavo, 15 in. quarto and 20 in. folio, and introduce additional sequences, with appropriate size symbols added to the location marks on the books and catalogue entries.

Pamphlets may be treated in several ways. Where these are numerous on a particular subject, it has been found satisfactory to store them in filing boxes arranged on the shelves, together with books on the same subject. Some of these in series, such as annual reports, will eventually be bound when there are enough to make a volume. Larger pamphlets may stand alone on the shelves, in one of the variety of pamphlet cases available. Rare and valuable items should be bound; if there are several on one subject, such as sermons or Civil War tracts, they might be bound in one volume; otherwise they should be treated separately, although this may necessitate bulking with blank pages. Bound volumes of miscellaneous pamphlets of assorted sizes are sometimes acquired as gifts; these are troublesome in many ways and are better broken up and each treated individually. Where there are too few items on a subject to justify the use of shelf space for filing boxes, or sizes are awkward, they may be conveniently stored in folders in vertical filing cabinets.

Periodicals may be stored in filing boxes and shelved with any bound volumes, together with other books on the subject, until a volume is complete, when it will be bound with title-page and index. Advertising matter should be bound in, for the information it contains is often as important to the subject as the text. Alternatively, simple folders may be made by pasting two pieces of card, slightly larger than the periodical, on a sheet of brown paper, leaving the width of a completed volume between them and flaps on the edges of one, to fold over the parts. Tapes are laced through the boards as ties and the title lettered on the paper spine.

At least two copies of local newspapers are required; one as a binding file and one for cutting and for use while the other is at the binders. The period covered by each bound volume will depend on the frequency of publication and the number of pages; volumes should not be too thick, both from the aspect of wear and of ease of handling. They should be stored horizontally, to avoid the sagging which damages large heavy volumes if shelved vertically. Wide shelves are required, of a depth to take only a small number of volumes for convenient handling and to reduce wear. It is preferable to avoid storage above average shoulder height. Incomplete files of early newspapers may be stored in boxes with hinged sides to open flat. Opportunities may occur to acquire missing issues and completed volumes may then be bound. The fragile condition of some early newspapers results in damage at each handling; this can be reduced by placing each issue in a folder, dated on the outside, although the bulk of the files is greatly increased. The safest course is to put them on microfilm for general use; the papers would then only need to be handled on rare occasions.

Newscuttings are most satisfactorily treated as separate items, mounted as columns on quarto sheets of stout paper. Sheets should have a printed heading ruled to take the subject heading, author if named, the source and date of the cutting and the filing mark. Lengthy cuttings may occupy more than one sheet; these should be stapled together, with the pages numbered and the heading repeated on each, in case of separation. Classification by subject, according to the scheme in use throughout the collection, is a convenient method of arrangement. The class number is used for filing and additions may be inserted in correct sequence. The cuttings may be filed in boxes, lettered with the class numbers included, and shelved as a sequence of volumes. In some cases, where a series of cuttings completes a subject, these may be mounted without headings, but with the source and date of each cutting added. With a title-page and contents list or index, they may be bound into a volume. These may include, for example, a series of articles on local buildings, villages or people; the writings of a local historian or extensive cuttings from local papers or elsewhere on some outstanding local event. Volumes of newscuttings are sometimes acquired as gifts. These have frequently been stuck in with no semblance of order and with no dating; valuable material is included, but its usefulness is limited by the difficulty of finding it. The work involved in removing the cuttings, dating them from internal evidence where possible, remounting and indexing them, would be repaid if time could be found to do it.

Unlike the maps in the general reference library, those in the local collection will not be discarded when they are out of date, but will be kept as historic records; their storage and preservation requires special consideration. Maps should be stored as issued, flat in the case of those printed on paper. Folded paper maps should be opened out and also stored flat, to avoid wear along the fold lines by constant use. Folded maps in directories become torn and damaged by being wrongly folded and are better removed and stored separately, a note being made in the book. The methods of storage most generally adopted are horizontally, in drawers, or vertically, in cabinets or by some method of suspension. Metal drawers are preferable to wood, being less liable to jam and more resistant to fire. Drawers should not be more than $2\frac{1}{2}$ in. deep for ease of handling the maps and to keep them to a manageable weight. Stiff folders may be used for subdividing the maps in each drawer, to facilitate finding and reduce unnecessary handling, and there should be a good clearance between the top of the maps in one drawer and the bottom of the one above. Cabinets for maps in frequent use should not be more than 5ft. high; they should, preferably, be of a height to enable the top to be used for consulting the maps. Vertical filing cabinets provide a convenient means of storing series of maps of uniform size, such as the Ordnance

Survey, where the sheet numbers used for arranging are readily seen. The recent practice of the Ordnance Survey in publishing two west/east adjoining sheets of the 25-inch series on one, necessitates filing these out of sequence and inserting references to their location. The Roneo-Vickers Planfile is fitted with curved dividers to hold the maps firmly in position; separators, wallets for holding small maps, to suspend on these and index labels are also supplied. Maps may also be stored horizontally on shelves in portfolios, with linen flaps and ties to exclude dust; boxes with hinged sides to open flat are convenient for small maps. Maps on rollers and extra large maps, rolled, should be stored in 'pipes' or given a protective cover and kept on racks or narrow shelves.

Paper maps in constant use need reinforcement to protect them for permanent preservation. They may be mounted on adhesive cloth by applying heat with a photographic mounting iron. Items needing surface protection may be similarly treated with 'Coverlon', a transparent plastic sheet. The use of rare and valuable maps should only be permitted with a protective transparent covering of polythene acetate; for general use of such maps, it is advisable to provide photocopies.

The illustrations collection will comprise several types, each requiring different treatment and method of storage, but whatever form is used, fittings should be of metal in preference to wood, to reduce fire risk. Photographs should be mounted on stiff paper mounts; a uniform size is convenient for storage in filing cabinets or boxes with hinged sides, arranged on shelves, and for readily locating a particular item. Mounts 10 in. × 12 in. accommodate most photographs; the number of larger ones in the collection will determine additional sizes used and alternative storage. Printed labels, with spaces for easily-read location mark, accession number, photographer, title, date and any other necessary information, pasted on the back of the mounts positioned in a top corner when filed, are an aid to speedy finding and replacement. Precautions against deterioration should be taken by the use of germ-free paste in mounting photographs, as all other material in the local collection. The approved recipe of 1 pound of best white flour, two pints of water and ¾ fluid ounce of formaldehyde should be used. The library might co-operate with a local record office in obtaining supplies of the recommended Canadian red wheat flour from a large mill. Prints and drawings should be stored horizontally in shallow-drawered cabinets, as for maps. They should not be mounted but may be placed in folders, perhaps 'windowed' and attached to the backing by transparent photo-corners, or they may be stored with tissues separating them in portfolios with dust-excluding flaps. According to size, several piles may be stored in each drawer, but, as with maps, there should be a good clearance between the drawers. Lantern slides, transparencies and photographic negatives should be placed separately in negative envelopes for protection, and stored in slide boxes. Brief identifying details may be written on the margins of lantern slides and negatives in white ink and on the mounts of transparencies; full descriptions may be given on the envelopes, with the class or other filing mark on the projecting top edge. Boxes, labelled with the contents, may be stored in a metal cupboard.

Broadsides should also be stored horizontally. Like maps, they will probably vary greatly in size and for economy of space and ease of handling, it may be necessary to arrange them in several sequences. They may be stored on shelves, in boxes or portfolios, or, as maps and prints, in metal drawers, with labelled dividers to reduce the wear and tear of handling. Dependent on the size of the collection, they may be classified as other material in the local collection or grouped under such subjects as crime, education, elections, theatres.

Due to their form, microfilms are not easily stored for quick identification. Storage in drawers or cabinets is wasteful of space unless the tins or boxes holding the reels are stacked, making access to a particular film difficult. Shallow boxes, taking one reel in depth and stored horizontally on shelves, are probably the most satisfactory arrangement. The contents of the boxes should be lettered on the back and details of each film written on the lid of the tin or top of the box, making them readily identified. At least the accession number should appear both on the reel and on the lead-in end of the film, where it can be written in white ink. It is necessary to remind readers that films must be rewound after use and to check that a film is on its correct reel when it is returned to the desk. Confusion can arise if this precaution is omitted. Short lengths of film, too small for tins or boxes, may be placed in folders and stored in suitable boxes with the others. Negatives should not be used for reading but should be stored for making possible copies. They should be checked every five years; traces of hypo, if left in processing, cause deterioration.

Gramophone records in the local collection will probably not be extensive. If the library has a record lending library, stout carrying cases will probably be provided; these would be suitable for storage in the local collection, vertically, on metal shelves. Where these are not available, shallow boxes slightly larger than the sleeves might be used. Accession numbers should appear on the sleeve and on the label of the record. Discs should be firmly, but not too tightly, packed with the contents of each case lettered on the spine. Storage in extreme temperatures should be avoided; 10° to 15° centigrade is the ideal. Tape-recordings should be stored in the same way as microfilms. Typewritten copies of some recordings, such as lectures, might usefully be made, put into covers or folders, and stored with pamphlets for use as other printed material. Reference to the typescript should be made on the tape.

Music scores, where possible, will be treated as books; they should be bound and shelved with the oversize books. Sheet music may be put into folders and either stored in boxes on the shelves or in a vertical filing cabinet together with pamphlets.

Manuscript letters will probably be afforded the protection of strong-room storage. They should be unfolded and stored flat in individual folders with a pocket to hold the letter firmly. Handling of letters may be reduced by including a typewritten

transcript with each, to be used for all general purposes. A brief
summary of the contents of letters, on the outside of the folders,
further avoids unnecessary handling. When used, letters should
not be exposed to a strong light and, as for valuable maps, the
surface should be protected by a transparent covering. Metal
boxes should be used for storage.

Apart from the measures to be taken for the safe storage and
convenient use of the collection already mentioned, other practices should be observed for the care and preservation of the
valuable material it contains. Irremediable damage can be done
by careless repairing. Tears should never be mended with adhesive tape; staff should be trained in correct methods. For
major repairs beyond their skill, expert advice should be sought.
This may be obtainable from a record office in the neighbourhood; otherwise, the Public Record Office will give advice and
carry out work. It has already been said that attention should
be paid to the heating and ventilation of storage space, and a
constant check should be kept for deterioration of any items.
Leather bindings are particularly vulnerable to modern heating
systems and should be regularly treated. The well-known
British Museum recipe is very satisfactory for this. Binding calls
for particular care. Rare books should be sent to a binder
specializing in restoration work, and as much of the old binding
as is possible should be retained, including endpapers. In some
cases it may be considered an act of vandalism to rebind a book,
such as an author's own copy of a first edition of an important
work. A box simulating a book, as near as possible to the original
binding, may be made to hold it. The current tendency to
dispense with instructions to the binder cannot obtain in the
local collection. Many books will have peculiarities requiring
individual attention and clear instructions should be given. The
wrappers and advertisements usually discarded in the binding
of periodicals are an essential part of the publication for local
collection purposes and should be retained. Bookplates, anno-
tated endpapers, papers loosely inserted, are among items which
add interest to the collection and which should be preserved if

rebinding is necessary. Rare and valuable items should not be defaced by stamping and lettering. Class numbers may be written on a small manilla tab, pasted inside the back board so that it projects above the pages just enough to be read. Process labels should not be stamped on the book, but on a slip of cartridge paper tipped to the endpaper at the joint. The librarian of the local collection will be very conscious of his responsibility for the safe keeping of the material in his charge and will be watchful for any means by which it may be harmed.

Chapter 8
Staff

STAFFING the local collection probably presents more problems than any other department of the library. The service relies more on personal assistance to readers than any other department, and the ability to provide that service is dependent on the staff. In addition to qualifications in librarianship they must be trained in the methods of historical study, with an ability to impart the information to others, and have an intimate knowledge of the material available if the fullest use is to be made of it. Statistics of issues, the factor commonly influencing establishment officers and others in the appointment of staff, provide little indication of the amount of work done by the staff of the local collection or of its value to the readers concerned, and the collection tends to be low on the list for the allocation of staff. Where it has been recognized that it is a special department and a member of staff (or an assistant) with specialist qualifications has been put in charge, members of the public have responded by availing themselves in increasing numbers of what it has to offer, and the reputation of the library service has been enhanced. Given the will to provide the department with adequate staff, there remains the problem of recruiting it.

Facilities for acquiring specialist qualifications for library work in the field of local history have increased during recent years. Additional to the courses in archive administration of the universities of Liverpool, London and Wales, the subject is included in the courses for degrees offered by the schools of librarianship of other universities and polytechnics and in the syllabus for the Library Association's General Professional and Post-Graduate Professional Examinations. Ideally, the librarian

of the local collection would be a graduate in history who had
also passed the Post-Graduate Examination of the Library
Association with the optional papers in Archive administration
and Literature and librarianship of local history but, before
embarking on such a course of study, he would need to be certain that this was the branch of the profession he wished to follow and that the chances of securing a post were reasonable. He
would probably elect to apply his skills in the record office
rather than in a library local collection, unless it was one of the
larger libraries, recognized as a record repository or otherwise
having a large accumulation of documents and including archivists on its staff. Similarly, the trainee library assistant or school-
leaver entering library school must have the same settled preference before embarking on his studies for the papers, in Part II
of the Library Association's General Professional Examination,
on the Library and local history, Archives and records management, Palaeography and diplomatic and Bibliographical organization of historical studies. It must be acknowledged that the
specialized nature of local collection work does not equip its
practitioners for the higher administrative posts of the profession,
and the ambitious young assistant who has set his sights high
may be reluctant to acquire, at the outset of his career, the
necessary specialist qualifications for what he may consider a
'dead-end' job. Neither may he be willing to stay long enough
in one place to gain the knowledge of its history which is an
essential part of the local collection librarian's equipment. The
local studies library is the place, rather, for those who are prepared to leave the race towards high places to others and pursue
the less ambitious course of enjoying, for its own sake, the
absorbing interest the job provides. Except in the larger libraries,
they must not expect to be among the most highly-graded members of the staff, for in the equation of responsibility, generally
according to the number of staff under supervision, they are
unlikely to rank very high.

Many local collections of long standing are manned by staff
who, like the writer, did not have the opportunity of including

specialist studies among their qualifications for librarianship, but were drafted into the department on account of their special interest or aptitude. Theirs has been in-service training, taking such opportunities as have presented themselves to acquire the necessary additional qualifications. There is a need for either part-time or full-time post-qualification courses in the librarianship of local studies. Apart from those who qualified before the present Library Association syllabus, the opportunity for further study should exist for assistants who, after some years of working in other departments, may find themselves attracted to local collection work. Those in the London area have the opportunity of taking the Diploma in History of the University of London Council for Extra-Mural Studies. Of the alternative schemes of study for this, one is concerned with local history; the course is in four parts, each occupying one year of part-time study. Enrolment may be for one year at a time, over an unlimited period, the final year being devoted to a piece of original work supervised by the lecturer. The Institute of Extension Studies of the University of Liverpool introduced at the beginning of the academic year 1972/73 a two-year part-time evening course leading to a Diploma in Local History. This is designed to give students the basic knowledge required to carry out research in local archives and to equip them with a background knowledge of at least three important periods in the history of Lancashire and Cheshire. In other places would-be students are not so well provided for but there are, increasingly, opportunities to attend short courses relevant to local studies organized by extra-mural departments of the universities, local authority colleges for further education and the Workers' Educational Association. These may include such subjects as the methods and materials of historical research, local administration and the records created, the religious, social and economic history of the area, a local industry, palaeography and heraldry. In many places groups are organized, under qualified tutors, for the study of some aspect of the area's history, based on records and other material in the local record office or libraries. Participation in such courses can provide valuable training for members of the local collection staff; the keen assistant will probably undertake this on his own initiative, but reimbursement of course fees and allowance of time off might well be considered by the employing authority as a recognized part of staff training. In recent years, many excellent books have been published on local and public records and their use as source material for the study of local history; by studying these and availing themselves of any facilities provided locally, the staff of the local collection can go a long way in furthering their professional education and acquiring the qualifications not achieved by examination.

Membership of the groups mentioned above will not only provide the librarian of the local collection with the knowledge essential for assisting his readers and for building up the collection, but will keep him in touch with all that is happening in the field of local studies in his area. He will know the participants, professional and amateur, and the subjects of their work; his interest will be good publicity for the library and will often be the means of acquiring for the collection a copy of a valuable piece of work which may never reach the stage of publication. He should also be an active member of the local branch of the *Historical Association* and of any other historical or literary societies concerned with matters of local interest. His membership may be personal, or he may be the library's representative by virtue of its institutional membership; he is likely to be invited to serve the society as an officer or committee member and to contribute to its affairs in such ways as reading papers or arranging exhibitions. All these activities will absorb a great deal of his off-duty time but will provide a means, in addition to the everyday handling of the material in the collection and his private reading, of acquiring the extensive knowledge of the history of the place which he must have.

Perhaps undue emphasis has been given to the requirements of the librarian in regard to local history. As has been stressed in earlier chapters, it is the function of the local collection to collect and make available materials on all spheres of activity within the area. Accordingly, the librarian must not concern himself solely with those whose interest is historical study; his interests must range widely and he must maintain contact with all groups within the community, know what they are doing and ensure that a record of their activities has its place in the collection.

In assembling, organizing and exploiting all the material to be used by the readers he is assisting, the librarian of the local collection, alone among his colleagues, has the opportunity of practising all the technical skills of librarianship which, no doubt, attracted him to the calling. The necessity of utilizing every item in the collection to its fullest capacity, requires the indexing, detailed cataloguing, and adaptations of classification which are not currently practised in centralized cataloguing departments. Knowledge of the subject and the uses to which material will be put necessitates these processes being carried out in the department. Furthermore, the close examination of the material in the course of these duties provides an invaluable knowledge of its content and resources. The librarian must also be a bibliographer; much of the material in the collection will have bibliographical interest in addition to its content value and he should be competent to deal with the enquiries he is likely to receive from the expert. He is also frequently liable to be called upon to give advice on old books and their value, not always books of local interest. He will know the wisdom of avoiding attempting to give valuations, but may be able to offer helpful advice. The writer has found it useful to keep a record of prices of local items realized at auction or quoted in booksellers' catalogues. Care and preservation of the material in his keeping is a further matter in which he must be practised. He must know and instruct his assistants in the use of the correct methods and materials for repair work and for storage. If the collection includes archives he will, doubtless, have mastered the art of their repair; in the collection where manuscripts are not numerous, such work is better given out to the expert.

The preparation of local history publications, which some

libraries undertake, requires the librarian to have the ability to write in a manner which will both convey information and arouse the interest of potential users of the collection. He must also be knowledgeable on methods of printing and lay-out and of reproduction work, call for a knowledge of design and the lay-out of exhibits and of the drafting of informative but concise labelling. Where the library is under joint directorship with the art gallery and museum, the writing of labels may be carried out by the display assistants, otherwise the librarian or his assistants will need to have the ability to do the work.

The local collection provides the best all-round training in librarianship for junior assistants. They will gain experience in cataloguing, classification and indexing, in the use of books and their care and preservation, in design and display work and, particularly, the art of finding out precisely what the enquirer wants to know and producing the material to meet his needs. In addition, they will learn something of the history of the place. It is common practice to move juniors from department to department; this is admirable for the purpose of their training but, for the purpose of staffing the local collection, their stay should be for a reasonable time. Perhaps more than most, the librarian of the local collection will be under-staffed; the training of assistants is time-consuming and he will not welcome the removal of an assistant when he is beginning to be an asset rather than something of a hindrance. In the course of such training, some young assistants may find an interest in the work which they may wish to pursue. It could influence them in their choice of subjects to be studied at library school, particularly if they could be assured of a post as a qualified assistant in the department on completion of the course.

The successful functioning of the local collection requires the constant attendance of staff qualified to deal with the needs of the many types of reader who make use of it. However detailed the catalogues and indexes, they can never supplant the knowledgeable assistant. Nothing can be more damaging to any institution's reputation than staff who neither know nor appear

4

to care about what is required of them. The librarian may have built up a fine collection, held in high repute in the area, but he cannot be in the library at all times. In his absence, the department should not be left in charge of some assistant it may be possible to spare from another section. It is unlikely that any local collection would fail to justify, by the amount of work necessary to maintain it, the appointment of at least one other full-time assistant who would be qualified to deputize for the librarian. If this is recognized and sufficient staff of the right quality provided, the collection will fulfil its purpose.

Chapter 9
Service to Readers

THE nature of its contents and the use to be made of them make it necessary for the local collection to be, principally, a reference library. Much of the material is unique and irreplaceable and should only be used under supervision. Further, it should be available whenever it is required, whether for quick consultation or prolonged study. It must be recognized, however, that the restriction of use to the opening hours of the library is often a serious handicap to the reader, whose work may be curtailed over the weekend or at night for lack of an essential book. Local students away at college or university, although at home during vacation, often need a book during term and requests are received from other libraries for books for students in their area. A good deal of material can be duplicated and whenever possible should be, to provide one copy available for loan. The facility of producing photocopies makes it possible to duplicate many unique items, such as theses. Multiple copies of some standard works, such as a town history for young readers, should be provided and issued for home reading. Such books should also be available at other libraries within the system. The ability to borrow from the local collection is not only an advantage to the reader; it is in the interests of the library, for it relieves what can often be a shortage of working space, and reduces the amount of unauthorized 'borrowing' which, unfortunately, takes place in spite of vigilance.

Where members of the public have access to the shelves, there can be no restriction as to admission for reference use, apart from rather unlikely exclusion under the by-laws, and no reader's ticket is required. It is desirable, however, to keep a check on everybody coming in. It has been found that a visitors' book, placed at the entrance to the department, requiring name and address and the subject of interest, proves a deterrent to any whose intentions may not be entirely lawful. It also provides a daily record of the use of the collection, necessary for the production of statistics to justify the existence of the service, but giving no true indication of its relative value.

The lending of material for home reading is unlikely to be extensive, so rules can be applied with some degree of flexibility. No special ticket should be required; in most cases the borrower will be a registered reader, either locally or of some other library whose tickets are acceptable for loans, and the production of a ticket will be his credential. The rare instances of a borrower not so registered make it unnecessary to maintain a borrowers' register in the local collection. In libraries where it is the practice to issue books immediately on completion of a borrower's application form, a book could be issued at the discretion of the librarian and the application form sent to the lending library for registration. The borrower's ticket could then be sent back to the local collection to await the return of the book. The recording of issues for home reading requires little organization; numbers are unlikely to justify other than the entry of details in a ruled book. The date of issue, class and accession numbers, author, title, borrower's name and address, date of any overdue notices sent, date of return and initials of the assistant receiving it are the essentials. Where the Browne charging system is in operation, the borrower's ticket can be filed, but in libraries operating photo or computer charging in the lending library, where the borrower needs to keep his ticket, a signature in the issue book might reasonably be required. Numbers of books issued and the period of loan are matters for discretionary adjustment. A high proportion of local collection readers are well known to the staff, appreciative of the value of the material in the collection and co-operative in its use. In some cases, material not normally available for home reading may be loaned overnight or for the weekend and such privilege is rarely abused. In others, extended loans may be made, subject to immediate return if requested. Material may sometimes be deposited in a university or college library, to be used under supervision, with precautions taken for its safe-keeping when not in use. Loans will probably also be made for official use by other departments of the local authority; these could generally be recalled at short notice if needed. The tendency to expect to have all the necessary material to hand over a long period should be discouraged, in the interests of other readers, by limiting the number of items allowed on loan at any time.

Issues of material used for reference can only be approximate-ly recorded where readers have access, if only partial, to the shelves. The common practice of notices requesting readers to leave books on the table after use, to be counted and shelved by the staff, is never reliable. Not all readers comply, and fre-quently a quick reference at the shelves satisfies an enquiry. A count of books left on the tables is no true record of the use made of them; some may have been closely studied, while others may have been scanned for information which the reader failed to find. Items produced on request can be recorded, but this may be misleading; a pile of loose-leaf newscuttings or of photographs, if individually counted, produce impressive statis-tics although they may have given the reader no more informa-tion than he might have found in a single book, had one been available on the subject. Library committees need to know the use that is being made of the services provided; issues, being the yardstick, must be recorded but they should be analysed by type of material and supplemented by reports on especially interesting or unusual enquiries.

As far as possible, readers should have access to the shelves. The library should be so arranged as to give complete oversight and staffing should be adequate to ensure that there is constant supervision. Many local collection readers are not always speci-fic in their requirements and the opportunity to explore is appreciated. Searches through a long run of directories, for example, would be intolerable for both reader and staff if each had to be requested and brought to the point of service. Much of the material, by its nature, will need to be closed to public access. Rare works, printed or in manuscript, early newspapers – often in a fragile condition – broadsides, photographs and micro-films are among the material for which restricted handling is desirable and which should be available only on request. Little-used items, such as a long run of council minutes, are better shelved apart, particularly if shelf space is limited in the public part of the library. It may also be an advantage to have a separate sequence of the duplicates available for home reading.

As in all departments of the library some rules will be neces-sary, but these should be only those required for safeguarding the collection, to prevent disturbance of other readers and to observe moral or legal obligations. Smoking and the use of ink are both hazards from which valuable and irreplaceable material must be protected. Tracing and copying are frequent requirements of local collection readers; they should be given all possible facilities for this, but regulation is essential. Maps and illustrations can be seriously damaged by tracing unless precautions are taken. Most readers recognize that tracing pub-lic property is not a right but a privilege, for which permission should be asked, although it would appear that many who guide the studies of the young and, sometimes, the not so young, fail to give this basic piece of instruction in the methods of collecting information. Transparent sheets of polythene acetate should be provided and if these are used under the tracing paper, with soft pencils, tracing can be safely permitted in most cases.

The facilities for photocopying which libraries are increasing-ly providing are reducing the amount of tracing necessary. Many types of machine are available, according to the prints they are required to produce. Some libraries have installed coin-operated machines such as those rented from Rank-Xerox or scm. These are limiting as to size of material they will take, but produce inexpensive copies suitable for most purposes and, particularly the scm, are easily operated by the public. Copies for schoolwork, for children and teachers, are sometimes charged at a reduced rate. Some authorities maintain a photographic section connected with the engineering or architectural department. These often have costly apparatus for the precise reproduction of plans, and other departments are encouraged to use the service provided. This can be used for work beyond the scope of the library's own equipment, such as enlargements and the reproduction of photographs. One library has been able to supply numbers of people in this way with excellent reproductions on heavy document paper of old prints, an inexpensive substitute for the rare originals. Requests are sometimes made for permission to photograph material with the reader's own equipment; providing this does not interfere with other readers, that acknowledgement is made and that there is no infringement of copyright, there is no valid reason for refusing. Local collections are sometimes called upon in this way to provide material for use in the production of television programmes having some connection with the locality. With the increase in the ownership of tape-recorders, recordings of passages from books and other material are replacing note-taking for many, and it is likely that increasing numbers of readers will want to use this means of gathering material. Again, if this can be done without disturbing other readers, it should be allowed.

When providing copies of any material for readers, the use to be made of it and the question of copyright must be borne in mind. Copyright in printed works lasts for fifty years, but copies of a reasonable amount may be made for research or private study. Only one copy of one article in a periodical may be made for any one student and from a book, only a 'reasonable proportion' may be reproduced, with the permission of the owner of the copyright. A photograph is copyright for fifty years after publication; if unpublished, for fifty years after the death of the photographer or the person who commissioned it. Ordnance Survey maps are Crown Copyright, which also lasts for fifty years after publication; old maps may be copied without restriction, but those in copyright may only be copied in part, for personal use by *bona fide* students. Copying is not permissible for use as legal evidence or in applications for planning permission. Copyright in manuscripts lasts for fifty years after the death of the author or one hundred years after they were written. If any copies made are intended for eventual publication, permission must be obtained from the owner of the copyright, except for short quotations, and the librarian of the local collection should be able to supply the reader with the necessary information to do this. A note of any conditions made by an author or depositor regarding the use of an unpublished work or document should be attached to it and strictly observed.

Some libraries limit the number of items a reader may have for use at any one time. Material for local studies is inclined to occupy a good deal of table space, particularly if several maps are being used for comparison together with other material, but the work being done may necessitate this and discretion should be exercised. Rare and valuable material should not be allowed to remain on the table when not actually in use; readers should be asked to return it to the staff desk immediately and the staff should make frequent checks of the tables and shelve for anything not in use.

Ideally, the local collection should be available at all times during the opening hours of the reference library, but this may not always be possible. Except in the larger libraries, staffing of the local collection is usually minimal. With only a small proportion having the specialist training required to give a satisfactory service and the need for constant supervision, the choice must be made between curtailing the hours of opening and leaving the department in the charge of untrained staff. In most places the greatest call on the service is likely to be during the working hours of schools and colleges, government, business and industry and on Saturdays and, if staff is not available to provide a good service at other times, it would appear reasonable to limit the service to when it is most needed. The reader who needs to work beyond the opening hours of the collection can be provided for by transferring the material he is using to the reference library. This requires some degree of supervision by the reference library staff and would not be practicable in the case of manuscripts and other rare material. Where the local collection is housed in the main reference library there will be no limitation of hours, although it will be necessary to provide for supervision of the use of rare material.

A great deal of staff time will be spent in assistance to readers. As all reference library staff know, enquirers are often uncertain about their requirements and unable to state them precisely. Much probing is often necessary to discover what is wanted; the intuitive sense that librarians tend to develop is frequently called into use. This is especially so in the local collection, where much depends on a knowledge of local affairs in the past and at the present time and on familiarity with the resources of the collection. However comprehensive the catalogues and indexes, these can never cover all the sources of information the collection includes; the personal knowledge of the staff will be necessary if it is to be fully exploited.

Students preparing to write a thesis or extended essay will need to know the material available on a proposed subject for submission to the tutor. In addition to gathering together everything in the collection relating to the subject, the librarian should be equipped with any bibliographies, calendars, catalogues or reports giving information about material on the subject available elsewhere. Whether or not it is on account of the reputation for service that libraries have earned, some students expect much of their work to be done for them. The Institute of Education of the University of Southampton is, it would appear, in the minority in advising students that they 'should not expect public officials such as librarians, archivists and museum curators to do it for them. They are busy people eager to help those who have helped themselves, but whose duties do not include planning essays for, and acting as research assistants to, students who visit them.' In practice, it is rarely the student who visits the library who is the offender; such requests are usually received by post and very often come from post-graduate workers. Although not within their duties, most local collection librarians, while suggesting that a visit is desirable, will provide details of any material on the subject likely to be available in the enquirer's area and offer to lend through the inter-library loan scheme anything available for home reading. It may be advisable, in the interests of local readers, to restrict such loans to one item at a time and to limit the period of loan.

'Environmental studies' in schools and colleges are largely dependent on a good local collection to supplement field work and visits to museums and other institutions and installations, and there is scope for much useful work in this direction. Success, however, depends very much on co-operative planning between the teacher or tutor and librarian. Many must have experienced the consternation caused by the unannounced arrival of a large party of children, all to do in the space of about an hour, some work requiring the use of the same material. The writer has known more than one such party in the library at the same time. Not only is it impossible to find working-space for them all, but with staff limited as it usually is, most of the time available to the children for working is spent in assembling material, in the intervals of attending to any other readers. This can be avoided if opportunities are made to gain the co-operation of the teachers. Talks to groups, arranged through the local branches of the teachers' unions or heads of colleges or, possibly, a letter sent to schools, with the approval of the Director of Education, can result in a planned approach to the work. Preliminary talks with the teachers and tutors on the subjects to be studied, the available material suited to the age-group concerned, the time of the visit and the number to be accommodated, enable a programme to be drawn up that will ensure that the necessary material is immediately available and that the session can be profitably spent. Many of the children, particularly of primary school age, have little knowledge of the use of books and it is often necessary for the staff to help them in finding and noting the information they require. There is considerable scope for co-operation with the local branch of the School Libraries Association, in giving talks on the local collection and instruction in the use of books and the preparation of 'jackdaws'. These, small collections of photocopies of pictorial, printed and, possibly, manuscript material relating to a local topic, can be valuable aids to the teaching of history and methods of study, but it must be emphasized that they should be used as an introduction to, and not a substitute for, the wider resources of the local collection.

Opportunities sometimes occur for similar collections to be displayed in the library, apart from the exhibitions which are a regular feature of the department's activities and which are dealt with elsewhere. Schools and colleges and groups such as Townswomen's Guilds or extra-mural classes sometimes ask for a visit to be arranged when members can see a collection of material on their subject and perhaps hear a short talk by the librarian. These may be on a local author, comprising the works in print or manuscript, biographies, portraits, letters and association items; the Civil War as fought in the area, with photographs of the places and portraits of local people involved, plans of battles and tracts; or on maps and mapmakers, showing the collection's examples of old and modern maps. Such displays provide an interesting introduction to source material and are often the starting point for further studies.

Answering telephone and postal enquiries accounts for a considerable part of local collection work. Telephone enquiries may be for readily-found information which can be given immediately or they may involve a long search of various sources. In the latter case, if the enquirer is local it will probably be necessary to ask him to come to the library to use the relevant material to be assembled in readiness. If the enquiry is from a distance, this is impracticable and, unless the matter is urgent, it is probably more satisfactory to answer by letter. Many librarians will undertake a considerable amount of searching to satisfy enquiries, but this may be open to abuse. Occasionally a reply brings further queries, with more to follow, and a halt has to be called when it becomes apparent that the library is acting as research agency to a professional historian. Postal enquiries often take the form of requests, usually from students or school-children, to send material on a given subject. In some cases it may be possible to pass the request to the information bureau or public relations department for publicity material to be sent, but generally a brief reading list, details of any material available for purchase and offers to supply photocopies or inter-library loans are all that can be provided. It is noticeable that offers involving payment are rarely taken up by such enquirers.

Requests are often received from other libraries for the loan of material in the collection. This may be for such items as the transactions of the local archaeological society, which are not, normally, available for loan. Most librarians will wish to accommodate colleagues, if only in the expectation of reciprocal service, and if possible will lend the volume to be used in the reference library. The alternative of supplying photocopies will be suggested, but for long articles the cost may be prohibitive. Loans for the use of county library readers raise the additional problem of there being no local library where the book might be used, thus necessitating a loan for home reading. In such cases it may be necessary to refuse to lend, while offering to supply photocopies. It will probably be necessary to limit the period of any loans made from the collection. The installation of Telex in many reference libraries has provided a means of speedy inter-library communication which can be a valuable asset to the local collection; apart from other advantages it can expedite loans.

Changes in the educational system and the increased opportunities for leisure-time activities are bringing more people to the study of local history. The local collection librarian should keep abreast of all developments in the field and adapt the service to meet the requirements of the increasing numbers who are becoming aware of what libraries have to offer in this direction.

Chapter 10
Extension Activities

THE local collection that has been systematically built up, organized and equipped for the use of all types of reader, whatever their line of enquiry, deserves to be used to its fullest capacity. Those who have discovered what it has to offer will make good use of it, and will provide much valued publicity, but there remain many who may believe that what they regard as a students' library is no place for them. It is for the librarian to let them know that this is not so; that there is in the local collection something relating to every sphere of activity in the locality, something of interest for everyone. The opportunities for him to make known the resources of the collection by taking it outside the confines of its usual abode both in deed and in word are manifold.

Publicity might begin within the library, directed to the reader who frequents one department only and, perhaps, has never thought that his interests might be served elsewhere. Posters will probably be displayed in all branch libraries and public departments, informing readers of all the other services the library provides. These must not be allowed to remain in the same place for long, becoming part of the fixtures, but should be changed frequently. A series advertising the local collection might be prepared for circulating throughout the system, each emphasizing some topic of interest covered by the collection and calling attention to the service available. Many borrowers at branch libraries in the outer suburbs are likely to be newcomers to the district; a display panel of material from the local collection on the area prior to development, perhaps including explanations for street names, may arouse their interest and induce them to pursue the subject further. Old prints and photographs never fail to attract, and the opportunity might be taken of giving an airing to the illustrations collection by displaying a small selection for a short time at branch libraries. A notice to the effect that these are a few from a large collection, will serve as an introduction to the local collection, particularly if it is made known that photocopies can be made available. Where the collection includes multiple copies of old prints, the growing practice of lending framed pictures for home decoration, at a charge, might usefully be extended to some of these.

Small displays in the entrance hall to the lending library and the main reference library, regularly changed, keep the local collection constantly in the public eye. A few carefully selected items, concisely labelled, with a brief account of the event featured, refers the onlooker to further material on the subject to be seen in the local collection, with details of its availability. The librarian of the widely-ranging local collection will never be at a loss to produce something of topical interest at all times. Anniversaries of local authors or other celebrities, such as a great actor or musician, provide an opportunity to show portraits, illustrations of the houses they lived in, their families and friends, manuscript letters, their works and material relating to places associated with them; to plays and the characters they made famous, together with programmes, playbills and theatres; scores, concert programmes and scenes. The anniversary of such a local historic event as a great battle might be the occasion for a commemorative display, or a national event, such as the Battle of Trafalgar, may have been fully reported in the local newspaper. This could be shown with a few appropriate items from other departments of the library. The building of a new railway station, or the closure of a line, gives a chance to show something on railway history; a visit by royalty, records of such visits in the past; an annual fair or festival, perhaps dating far back, would produce material of interest. A general election might be an appropriate time to display cartoons, lampoons and poll books relating to elections of the past. If any of the items shown were acquired as gifts, this might usefully be noted; such publicity provides a strong inducement to others who may have in their possession something of value to the collection.

Reproductions of illustrations from the local collection might be used to give added interest to bulletins, annual reports or other publications of the library. A short historical note on the subject of the illustration, perhaps giving sources of the information, calls attention to the collection, and a note might be added to the effect that offers of material, as gifts or to purchase, would be welcome. Many libraries produce publicity leaflets for distribution to teachers, local societies and institutions and to postal enquiries. These are sometimes general, but are often concerned with individual departments. Such a leaflet would provide a ready reply to many of the postal enquiries received for material from the local collection. It might list the subjects covered, the types of material, their availability, the location of the collection and the hours of opening, and details about any special collections and any publications for sale.

Advantage should be taken of every opportunity that occurs to co-operate with other bodies in exhibiting items from the collection, bringing its resources to the notice of a wider audience than the library may command. A civic theatre might hold an exhibition in the foyer on theatrical history, in connection with a gala opening of a new season. Contributions from the library's collection could include playbills, programmes, illustrations of earlier theatres, press notices and photographs of actors. Many places have active local centres of the National Trust. Material on Trust properties in the neighbourhood, and the families who had lived there, might be provided from the local collection to supplement the Trust's publications at an exhibition designed to recruit members. Examples of various types of material might be included, as sources of history, in an exhibition arranged in conjunction with the local branch of the Historical Association, to celebrate some landmark in its history. A musical festival might be the occasion for an exhibition on the history of music and music-making in the area, held either in the museum or in the theatre or concert hall where the events take place. Instruments from the museum's collection could be shown together with printed, manuscript and pictorial material from the local collection. A local shop, celebrating its jubilee or centenary by a window display, might re-create the atmosphere of its early days by incorporating enlarged photographs of contemporary street scenes from the library's illustrations collection. In loaning valuable material for exhibition outside the library premises, it will need to be adequately insured and suitable provision made to ensure its safety.

In all places, there will be events from time to time providing the occasion for more extensive exhibitions of the material in the local collection. Where there is a museum or art gallery, such an exhibition may be held there, with its staff responsible for the mounting. The event should be widely publicized, with invitations to bring parties being sent to bodies for whom the exhibition may have an especial interest. An exhibition was held in the Art Gallery at Coventry, arranged by the art director and his staff, with material from the local collection illustrating George Eliot's association with the town, as part of a programme of events celebrating the 150th anniversary of her birth. Another similarly arranged exhibition marked the centenary of the public library there. Exhibition halls are sometimes found in association with the architectural and planning department; these may be let to other bodies and their siting in a busy thoroughfare would provide an opportunity for the library to put on an occasional display to catch the attention of passers-by.

The friendly relations usually existing between the library and the local press can be turned to good account on behalf of the local collection. A word to the effect that a display is currently to be seen on some matter of topical interest will generally result in a report being given. The staff of the local newspaper are often very dependent on the local collection; if a reputation has been built up for painstakingly providing the answers to enquiries the collection will be much relied upon, but the service given will be repaid by the publicity it will receive. A report on some local matter which has been the subject of an enquiry or controversy, will usually give acknowledgement for information supplied by the local collection in providing an answer. Letters to the editor frequently present an opportunity for publicizing the collection. Some event may prompt a reader to enquire or reminisce on a similar event in the past. The collection will probably include newscuttings or other material which answers the enquiry or corrects a faulty recollection; a letter sent to the newspaper on the subject will usually be published, and will often bring other interested readers into the library. In the event of some acquisition of especial interest, such as a collection of photographic negatives or of cuttings books, the paper would probably report this or publish an article on it contributed by the librarian. He may be invited to write an occasional article of topical interest, such as on early local newspapers at the time when their survivor is celebrating its centenary. He will probably also be called upon to check local historical information in such publications as a yearbook issued by the local newspaper.

The librarian of the local collection will usually not lack opportunities to talk about the collection and the information it provides. Groups of people exist in all places for a multiplicity of purposes; all are on the constant look-out for speakers and many are interested in the history of the area and in knowing what services are available within the community. Talks may either be about the collection and the material it includes, or about some aspect of local history to be gathered from it. Schools and colleges, and study groups of such organizations as Townswomen's Guilds and Women's Institutes can be informed of the wide resources of the collection and the use they may be able to make of it. Other groups, such as Senior Citizens, are primarily interested in hearing about the history of the place; its old buildings, surviving customs, the people commemorated by monuments in public places, the industries that once provided the place with its livelihood. Where possible, the collection's slides and photographs might be used in illustration.

Whatever the nature of the talk, it should be borne in mind that its purpose is not the provision of gratuitous entertainment but publicity for the local collection, and the occasion should be used to display or mention the sources from which the matter of the talk was gleaned.

A number of libraries produce their own pamphlets on local history topics; these are useful in providing both a short account of the subject and a bibliography for the guidance of readers wishing to pursue the matter further. Coventry's series of pamphlets had a fortuitous beginning. Constantly recurring enquiries were received, from all over the country and overseas, for information on a number of subjects associated with the city's history. Replying to these entailed the writing of many long letters, until it was decided to produce a once-for-all compilation on each, including a brief bibliography, to be sent to enquirers. The Corporation printing and stationery department print these by off-set litho, with a type-set cover having an appropriate illustration. They have a ready sale and several reprints have been necessary, in particular of the one on silk ribbon pictures. A series of reproductions of historic maps was similarly begun to meet a demand. An enlarged photocopy of Speed's map of Coventry, used to illustrate a talk given to numerous groups, produced frequent requests for copies. It was found that a printed reproduction, much superior, could be sold at a fraction of the price of the photocopy. The initial printing sold out within a few weeks and it, and the others later added, together with Buck's prospect, have also been reprinted several times. Prints and photographs from the illustrations collection, reproduced as Continental-sized postcards and sold packeted in sets of six, have had a steady demand for a number of years. They are used by students and schoolchildren as illustrations to local projects, bought by tourists, sent to relatives overseas and are avidly collected by local citizens, who frequently ask for more to be produced.

In historic towns with a thriving tourist industry, there is a great demand for brief information on many matters of local interest. Local ceremonies, customs and sayings, coats of arms, monuments, street names, city walls and gates are among the matters that interest visitors. Duplicated leaflets, compiled from material in the local collection, for sale at the information bureau or other suitable places, provide one means of meeting this demand.

It should be the aim of the library service to make its local collection the focal point for all matters of local interest. The resources of the collection must be made known to all whom it may benefit; it should be the place to which all members of the community should automatically address their enquiries on any matter concerning the locality. The best publicity the department can gain is by not only endeavouring to meet the demands put upon it, but by anticipating and creating demands and making provision to meet them.

Select Bibliography

Select Bibliography

BOUWENS, BETHELL G. *Wills and their whereabouts.* 1939.
BRITISH RECORDS ASSOCIATION. 'The ideal lay-out of a local record repository.' (In *Archives,* No. 6, 1951 and No. 6, 1952.)
BURKE, A. M. *Key to the ancient parish registers of England and Wales.* 1908
BURKETT, J. *Microrecording in libraries.* Library Association, 1957.
BURKETT, J. AND MORGAN, T. S. ed. *Special materials in the library.* Library Association, 1963.

CARTER, G. A. 'Libraries and local history' (In *The Librarian and Book World.* August and September 1955).
CELORIA, FRANCIS. *Teach yourself local history.* English Universities Press, 1959.
COLLISON, R. L. *The treatment of special materials in the library,* ASLIB, 1955.
CONDIT, LESTER. *A pamphlet about pamphlets.* Univ. of Chicago Press, 1939.

DOUCH, ROBERT. *Local history and the teacher.* Routledge & Kegan Paul, 1967.

ELLIS, ROGER. 'Local history, archives and libraries'. (In *Proceedings of the Annual Conference of the Library Association, Scarborough,* 1960, pp. 9–15.)
EMMISON, F. G. *Archives and local history.* Methuen, 1966.
ESCREET, P. K. *Introduction to the Anglo-American Cataloguing Rules.* Deutsch, 1971
ESDAILE, A. *Student's Manual of Bibliography.* Allen & Unwin, 1967.

FINBERG, H. P. R. *The local historian and his theme.* Leicester, 1952.
FOSTER, C. W. *Local history, its interest and value.* Lincoln, Lindsey Local History Society, 1950.
FOWLER, G. HERBERT. *The care of county manuscripts.* 3rd ed., 1939.

GALBRAITH, V. H. *The public records.* OUP, 1934.

GILSON, J. P. *A student's guide to the manuscripts of the British Museum.* SPCK, 1920.

GUISEPPI, M. S. *A guide to the manuscripts preserved in the Public Records Office.* 2 vols. 1923.

HARLEY, J. B. AND PHILLIPS, C. W. *The historian's guide to Ordnance Survey maps.* National Council of Social Service, 1964.

HEPWORTH, PHILIP. *Archives and manuscripts in libraries.* Library Association, 1958.

HISTORICAL ASSOCIATION. *English local history handlist.* G. Philip & Son, 1952.

HOBBS, JOHN L. *Libraries and the materials of local history.* Grafton, 1948.

HOBBS, JOHN L. *Local history and the library.* Completely revised and partly rewritten by George A. Carter. Deutsch, 1973.

HOBBS, JOHN L. 'Local records and the library'. (In *The Library Association Record*, Vol. 51, No. 6, 1949).

HOBBS, JOHN L. ed. *The Librarian and Book World.* Double number: 'Local collections', September–October, 1955.

HOSKINS, W. G. *English local history: the past and the future.* University Press, Leicester, 1967.

HOSKINS, W. G. *Fieldwork in local history.* Faber, 1967.

HOSKINS, W. G. *Local history in England.* Longmans, 1959.

HUMPHREYS, D. W. *Local history in school: a guide for teachers and students.* Standing Conference for Local History, 1953.

JENKINSON, SIR HILARY. *A manual of archive administration.* Lund, Humphries, 1965.

JOHNSON, CHARLES. *The care of documents and the management of archives.* SPCK, 1919.

LANGWELL, W. H. *The conversation of books and documents,* Pitman, 1957.

LE HARDY, WILLIAM. 'Records of local clubs and societies'. (In *Archives,* No. 3, 1950).

LIBRARY OF CONGRESS. *Notes on the cataloguing, care and classification of maps and atlases.* 1921.

MASON, DONALD. *Document reproduction in libraries.* AAL, 1968.

MICROCARD EDITIONS INC. *Guide to microforms in print.* Washington, DC, 1961–.

NATIONAL COUNCIL OF SOCIAL SERVICE. *Introducing local history.* 1960.

ORMEROD, JAMES. *How to catalogue a local collection.* C. Combridge, 1933.

OVERINGTON, MICHAEL A. *The subject departmentalized public library.* Library Association, 1969.

PAGE, S. B. *Modern office copying.* Deutsch, 1966.

PLENDERLEITH, H. J. *The conversation of prints, drawings and manuscripts.* British Museum, 1937.

REDSTONE, LILIAN J. AND STEER, FRANCIS W. eds. *Local records: their nature and care.* G. Bell & Sons, 1953.

SAVAGE, E. A. *Special librarianship in general libraries, and other papers.* Grafton, 1939.

SAYERS, W. C. BERWICK. *Library local collections.* Allen & Unwin, 1939.

VERRY, H. R. *Document copying and reproduction processes,* Fountain Press, 1958.

WALTON, MARY. *Local records and the public library.* (Unpublished thesis accepted for the Honours Diploma of the Library Association. Copy in LA library).

WARDLE, D. B. *Document repair.* Society of Archivists, 1971.

Index

Index